—

THE ESSENTIAL BIBLE
SURVEY OF THE OLD TESTAMENT

Copyright © 2003 Angus Hudson Ltd/Tim Dowley & Peter Wyart trading as Three's Company

Text ©1988, 1993 by Paul N. Benware
ISBN 0-8024-24821-1

First published in the USA
by Moody Publishers, Chicago

Worldwide co-edition organized and produced by Angus Hudson Ltd, Concorde House, Grenville Place, Mill Hill, London NW7 3SA, England
Tel: +44 20 8959 3668
Fax: +44 20 8959 3678
e-mail: coed@angushudson.com

All Scripture quotations, unless otherwise indicated, are taken from the New American Standard Bible®, © Copyright The Lockman Foundation 1960, 1962, 1963, 1968, 1971, 1972, 1973, 1975, 1977, 1995. Used by permission.

Library of Congress Cataloging-in-Publication Data

Benware, Paul N., 1942–
Survey of the Old Testament / by
Paul N. Benware.
1 2 3 4 5 6 07 06 05 04 03
Printed in Singapore

Picture Acknowledgments

Photographs
Tim Dowley: pp. 1, 3, 11, 46, 54, 65, 79, 81, 83, 94, 109, 112, 114, 119, 123, 126, 163, 165, 171, 172, 175, 177, 179, 185, 189, 195, 200, 201, 205, 207, 208, 215, 219, 232, 246, 249, 251, 263
Israel Government Tourist Office: p. 183
Peter Wyart: pp. 27, 29, 71, 88, 99, 105, 129, 152, 167, 169, 176, 192, 210, 234, 238, 243, 253, 257, 261

Illustrations
Alan Harris: p. 198
James Macdonald: pp. 9, 37, 74
Richard Scott: p. 155

Maps
Hardlines

Charts and Graphics
Peter Wyart

Moody Publishers, a ministry of the Moody Bible Institute, is designed for education, evangelization, and edification. If we may assist you in knowing more about Christ and the Christian life, please write to us without obligation:

Moody Publishers, c/o MLM, `
Chicago, Illinois 60610 USA

THE ESSENTIAL BIBLE
SURVEY
OF THE
OLD TESTAMENT

PAUL N. BENWARE

MOODY PUBLISHERS
CHICAGO

Contents

Index of Graphics

To
my Old Testament students
at Moody Bible Institute—

together pursuing the wisdom of God

PART 1

Introduction and Overview

1. *Introduction*
to the Old Testament

THE IMPORTANCE OF STUDYING THE OLD TESTAMENT

A person will never properly understand the New Testament Scriptures if the Old Testament Scriptures remain a mystery to him. Yet for the average Christian the pattern, unity, and progression of the Old Testament remain vague or unknown. Although almost everyone knows about Noah and the ark, Moses and the Red Sea, and numerous other stories found in the books of the Old Testament, the Old Testament itself often seems fragmented and is seen only as a loosely knit group of stories. But to understand God's ways and His purposes in this age, as well as His plans for the future ages, requires a clear comprehension of the Old Testament.

For example, there are about 350 direct quotes or clear allusions from the Old Testament found in the New Testament book of Revelation.[1] This amounts to about fifteen Old Testament references per chapter. It is no wonder that for many who do not have a good grip on the Old Testament, Revelation is essentially a closed book. Or who can really appreciate the apostle Paul's discussion about Israel in Romans 9–11 if there is no understanding of Genesis 12 and Jeremiah 31? Comprehending the Old Testament is crucial to understanding the New Testament.

Sculpture of the Ten Commandments.

Order and Classification of the Books of the Old Testament

THIS STUDY	STANDARD ENGLISH CLASSIFICATION	HEBREW CLASSIFICATION
Foundational Books	**Books of the Law**	**The Law**
Genesis	Genesis	Genesis
Exodus	Exodus	Exodus
Numbers	Numbers	Leviticus
Joshua	Deuteronomy	Numbers
Judges	**Books of History**	Deuteronomy
1 Samuel	Joshua	**The Former Prophets**
2 Samuel	Judges	Joshua
1 Kings	Ruth	Judges
2 Kings	1 Samuel	Ruth
Ezra	2 Samuel	1 Samuel
Nehemiah	1 Kings	2 Samuel
Complementary Books	2 Kings	1 Kings
Leviticus	1 Chronicles	2 Kings
Deuteronomy	2 Chronicles	**The Latter Prophets**
Ruth	Ezra	Isaiah
1 Chronicles	Nehemiah	Jeremiah
2 Chronicles	Esther	Ezekiel
Esther	**Books of Poetry/Wisdom**	Hosea
Books of Poetry/Wisdom	Job	Joel
Job	Psalms	Amos
Psalms	Proverbs	Obadiah
Proverbs	Ecclesiastes	Jonah
Ecclesiastes	Song of Solomon	Micah
Song of Solomon	**The Major Prophets**	Nahum
Lamentations	Isaiah	Habakkuk
Prophets During the Divided Kingdom	Jeremiah	Zephaniah
Obadiah	Lamentations	Haggai
Joel	Ezekiel	Zechariah
Jonah	Daniel	Malachi
Amos		
Hosea		
Isaiah		
Micah		

THIS STUDY	STANDARD ENGLISH CLASSIFICATION	HEBREW CLASSIFICATION
Prophets During the Single Kingdom	**The Minor Prophets**	**The Writings**
Nahum	Hosea	Psalms
Zephaniah	Joel	Job
Jeremiah	Amos	Proverbs
Habakkuk	Obadiah	Ruth
Prophets During the Exile	Jonah	Song of Solomon
Daniel	Micah	Ecclesiastes
Ezekiel	Nahum	Lamentations
Prophets After the Exile	Habakkuk	Esther
Haggai	Zephaniah	Daniel
Zechariah	Haggai	Ezra
Malachi	Zechariah	Nehemiah
	Malachi	1 Chronicles
		2 Chronicles

Great doctrinal truths are developed in the Old Testament. For example, significant revelations concerning the attributes of God are recorded. The New Testament, of course, concerns itself with the Person of God, but it is the Old Testament that gives us our basic understanding of God's majesty, power, holiness, and sovereignty. His love, goodness, and wisdom are the subjects of many psalms and numerous prophetic declarations. What can rival Isaiah 40 on the greatness of God or Psalm 23 on the loving care of God?

Perhaps it is our lack of understanding of the Old Testament that has brought about a basic deficiency in our knowledge of God and, as a result, our walk with Him.

The Church has surrendered her once lofty concept of God and has substituted for it one so low, so ignoble, as to be unworthy of thinking, worshiping men. . . . The low view of God entertained almost universally among Christians is the cause of a hundred lesser evils everywhere among us. A whole new philosophy of the Christian life has resulted from this one basic error in our religious thinking.[2]

After serious study of the Old Testament, one is inclined to walk with more reverence before our majestic God.

So much foundational truth is found in the Old Testament— truth that the New Testament writers assume we know and understand. An almost endless list of doctrinal truths and meaningful facts could be given to validate the importance of the Old Testament to the New. Yet so often, students of the Scriptures wrestle with truth found in the books of the New Testament because they fail to recognize Old Testament background.

THE PURPOSE OF THIS SURVEY BOOK

The purpose of this study is to assist the Bible student in seeing the pattern, progression, and unity of the Old Testament Scriptures and to be able to think through the entire Old Testament. A person must see the "big picture," and then he can begin to relate the various parts to this comprehensive view. Also, it is the purpose of this book to develop the central, unifying theme of the Old Testament, which is God's covenant promises to the nation of Israel.

THE APPROACH OF THIS SURVEY BOOK

The Old Testament is made up of thirty-nine books. These books contain the history of the nation of Israel, the laws of God for Israel, insightful and inspiring poetry, and the messages of numerous prophets. To observe how these books relate to one another our study will begin with and will emphasize the eleven "foundational books." These eleven books develop the story line of the Old Testament. Since these foundational books form the chronological and historical basis for the other twenty-eight books, the great emphasis in this study of the Old Testament will be placed on them. Once we work our way through the foundational books, the other books will be linked to this historical base. This approach will aid in our awareness of the pattern and progression of the Old Testament Scriptures (see chart "Order and Classification of the Books of the Old Testament," pages 12–13).

Another emphasis of this study will be to develop the central, unifying theme of the Old Testament, which is God's covenant promises to Abraham and his descendants. God's great covenant promises to Israel are the "glue" that holds the Old Testament together. In fact, the whole of the Bible is unified by God's covenant relationship with Israel, which also includes the Gentiles. It is unlikely that a full comprehension of the "New" covenant, based on the death of Jesus Christ, can exist without understanding its Old Testament context.

When the chronological framework is understood and the unifying theme is observed, the Old Testament makes sense. The fragmentation is gone, and the unity, pattern, and progression can be appreciated.

2. Overview
of the Old Testament

The Old Testament is the story of the nation of Israel, a nation unique and distinct from all the nations of the earth because God Himself entered into a covenant relationship with them. It is the story of a nation designed by God to bring glory to Himself and salvation to mankind—a story of the great spiritual victories and defeats of men and the amazing faithfulness and grace of God.

GOD'S DEALINGS WITH MANKIND

The Old Testament is divided into two distinct parts, each covering several thousand years of history. The first is Genesis 1–11 and is a record of God's dealings with mankind generally. During those years, there was no special group such as the church or the nation of Israel. God's dealings were with individuals. Since we do not know the exact date of the creation of the universe, we cannot say with certainty, as some do, that Genesis 1–11 covers two thousand years. It could be several thousand years more (but not millions or billions of

years). Much is not recorded about these early years of man, but four important events are included—the creation account, the Fall of man, the great Flood of Noah's day, and the division of mankind at the Tower of Babel. These events are briefly recorded so that we understand where this material universe came from, where sin and evil came from, and why the world of mankind is so fragmented. But the first few thousand years of human history are passed over quickly in order to get to the main emphasis of the Old Testament, which is the selection of Israel as God's chosen nation.

GOD'S DEALINGS WITH ISRAEL

The second distinct part of the Old Testament covers about 2,000 years. This part begins with Genesis 12 and includes all the rest of the Old Testament. Genesis 12 is the cornerstone chapter of the Bible. It is here that God selects a man by the name of Abraham and enters into an eternal, unconditional covenant with him and his descendants. God made many promises to Abraham. These promises included personal blessings to Abraham and his descendants and blessings that would include all the rest of mankind.

The Abrahamic Covenant

In this covenant, God promised that from Abraham He would make a great nation. The first four foundational books (Genesis, Exodus, Numbers, and Joshua) record the formation of the nation of Israel. In order to have a nation, three basic elements must be present—*people, law,* and *land.*

Genesis 12–50 records how God began to populate this new nation. In these chapters God's dealings with Abraham and his family make it abundantly clear to all that God is the giver of life and He guarantees the "people element" of a nation. When Genesis ends the nation has grown to about seventy-five people, which is not usually thought of as a "great" nation. But during the 275 years between Genesis and Exodus, a population explosion took place. By the Exodus, the nation's population had grown to more than 2 million. The *people* element of the nation was completed.

The Mosaic Law

Next, in order to function as a legitimate nation, Israel needed a code of *laws* to live by. Israel had become enslaved to the Egyptians during the period between Genesis and Exodus, but was miraculously set free by God and His human leader Moses. After their mighty deliverance, recorded in the book of Exodus, the people of Israel journeyed to Mount Sinai, where they received their constitution, laws covering all aspects of life. They camped at Mount Sinai for about a year, receiving the law and constructing their portable worship center, the Tabernacle.

The Promised Land

When the year at Mount Sinai was completed, Israel left to possess the Promised Land, the land of Canaan. This land was part of the covenant God had made with Abraham about four hundred years before. With the taking of this *land,* the third and last element would be fulfilled, and Israel would begin her role as a "great" nation. However, the third foundational book, Numbers, records a terrible moment in Israel's history. At that time, Israel refused to believe and obey God, which kept her from possessing the land. Instead of living in Canaan, Israel wandered aimlessly in a wilderness region for almost forty years.

When that period of discipline was over, Israel headed to the east side of the Jordan River and prepared to cross into her land. It was at this time that Israel's great leader Moses died. Just before Moses' death, God chose Joshua to lead the nation. He led Israel across the river and into the land of the wicked Canaanites. He directed the armies of Israel in the destruction of the main strongholds of the Canaanites. This period of warfare lasted from five to seven years. With the breaking of Canaanite power, the people of Israel could lay claim to the entire land. Israel now had people, laws, and a land. The period of the formation of the nation was over (see chart "Eras of Old Testament History," page 21).

Joshua then divided the land, giving each of

Israel
The Promised
Land

Tyre

PLAIN OF PHOENICIA

Dan

Mt. Hermon
(9,232ft / 2,184m)

Lake Huleh

SYRIAN DESERT

Acco

Hazor

A R A M

GREAT SEA
(MEDITERRANEAN SEA)

Mt. Carmel
(1,732ft / 528m)

Tiberias

SEA OF CHINNERETH
(SEA OF GALILEE)

Mt. Tabor
(1,929ft / 588m)

Yarmuk

PLAIN OF SHARON

VALLEY OF JEZREEL

Megiddo

Mt. Gilboa
(1,630ft / 497m)

Pella

G I L E A D

Jordan

Mt. Ebal
(3,083ft / 940m)

Samaria

Shechem

Jabbok

Joppa

I S R A E L

Mt. Gerizim
(2,889ft / 881m)

HILLS OF EPHRAIM

Shiloh

A M M O N

Lod

Bethel

THE ARABAH

Gezer

Gibeon

Jericho

Jerusalem

Mt. of Olives
(2,723ft / 830m)

Heshbon

PLAIN OF PHILISTIA

Bethlehem

Mt. Nebo
(2,630ft / 802m)

elon

SHEPHELAH

J U D A H

WILDERNESS OF JUDEA

Gaza

Lachish

HILLS OF JUDEA

Hebron

SALT SEA (DEAD SEA)

Dibon

Arnon

M O A B

Beersheba

T H E   N E G E B

Zered

THE ARABAH

E D O M

metres	feet
1,000	3,281
500	1,640
200	656
0	0
below sea level	below sea level

0   25   50 km

0   10   20   30 miles

Chronological Relationships of Old Testament Books

Archaeological excavations on the site of the ancient city of Jericho, near the Dead Sea.

the twelve tribes of Israel a clearly delineated area. It was now the task of each individual tribe to complete the conquest of the land by eliminating every single Canaanite living in its tribal area. God had specifically commanded them not to intermarry with the Canaanites, not to make treaties with them, and not to allow any to live among them. Unfortunately, Israel once again chose not to obey.

The National Rulers

When Joshua died, Israel entered a new era in its national life. God did not replace Joshua with a new leader for His people. It was God's intention that the newly formed nation be a theocracy (God ruling) with no single human leader. God would govern through the law given at Sinai and through the priests as the interpreters and enforcers of the law. But the theocracy turned out to be a failure because Israel would not obey her own constitution. The fifth foundational book, Judges, records these years, known primarily for their defeat and failure. During the more than three hundred years of the theocracy, judges had to be raised up again and again in crisis situations. The judges would deliver Israel from her enemies and bring in a time of obedience and peace. But those times eventually gave way once again to sin, unbelief, and idolatry. Another judge would be raised up by God, and the cycle would repeat itself.

After three centuries of repeated failure,

Eras of Old Testament History

2090 B.C.

ABRAHAM

1. Era of Formation

715 years
1. People
2. Law
3. Land

1375 B.C.

JOSHUA

2. Era of Theocracy

332 years
1. Priest
2. Judges

1043 B.C.

SAUL

3. Era of Monarchy

457 years
1. United
2. Divided
3. Single

586 B.C.

JEREMIAH

4. Era of Restoration

156 years
1. Captivity
2. Return

430 B.C.

NEHEMIAH

Israel demanded a human king. Even though this was a repudiation of God's rulership, He allowed Saul to become Israel's first king. With Saul's coronation Israel entered a third era in her history—the period of the monarchy. The next four foundational books (1 and 2 Samuel, 1 and 2 Kings) record the next 450 years of Israel's history. First and 2 Samuel tell the stories of Israel's first king, Saul, and Israel's greatest king, David. It was with King David that God made a marvelous covenant, much of which is fulfilled in David's "great son," the Lord Jesus Christ. David's son Solomon reigned after the death of David and was the third and last king to rule over all of Israel's twelve tribes.

The Divided Nation

Because of Solomon's sinful ways, God judged the family of David by dividing the nation into two separate kingdoms. The Northern Kingdom, Israel, consisted of ten tribes. The Southern Kingdom was called Judah and was made up of two tribes ruled by the family of David. For two centuries these two kingdoms coexisted, sometimes as friends and other times as foes. But the time of the divided kingdom came to an end when, because of sin and idolatry, the Northern Kingdom was destroyed by the nation of Assyria. The Southern Kingdom existed alone for more than one hundred years. It lasted longer because it was blessed with the presence of some godly kings. But, like the North, the Southern Kingdom went into idolatry. This time God used the nation of Babylon as His rod of discipline. Many people from the Southern Kingdom, including Daniel and Ezekiel, were deported from Judah to Babylonia. The nation lived in captivity for about seventy years.

The Partial Restoration

Finally, in fulfillment of His promise, God restored many of the people to their own land. The final period in the Old Testament history of Israel is recorded in Ezra and Nehemiah, the final two foundational books. This 150-year period focuses on both the political and spiritual restoration of Judah, and on several great men who were used in that restoration.

With the end of the book of Nehemiah, the story of the Old Testament comes to a close. Some four hundred years would go by before the Scriptures would pick up the story again. The years of silence would be broken by an angelic messenger, Gabriel, who would announce the birth of John the Baptist and the birth of Jesus the Messiah, the "great son" of David. God had not forgotten or gone back on His covenant promises to Abraham and his descendants.

This is a brief overview of the basic story of the Old Testament. Now our task is to look with greater care at each of the foundational books and then link to them the rest of the books of the Old Testament.

PART 2
The Foundational Books

3. *Genesis*

INTRODUCTION TO GENESIS

Authorship and Date of Genesis

The book of Genesis is part of the sacred Scriptures. Ultimately, therefore, God is the author and the source of all this recorded truth. Every Scripture is "God-breathed" (2 Tim. 3:16). But God did employ men to write down His message. Each human author used his own writing style, vocabulary, background, and personality as he wrote the truth of God. These men were "carried along" by the Holy Spirit of God in their efforts (2 Pet. 1:20–21), thus guaranteeing the accuracy and the authority of the writings. Genesis and the other Old Testament books are, therefore, documents with dual authorship—God's and man's.

Moses was the human author of Genesis and the other books of the Pentateuch. (*Pentateuch* is a Greek word commonly used for the first five books of the Old Testament.) These five "books of the Law" were written by Moses alone, with the exception of Deuteronomy 34, which records the death of Moses. (For a further discussion of the Mosaic authorship of Genesis and the rest of the Pentateuch, see "The Mosaic Authorship of the Pentateuch," page 49.)

The writing of Genesis, and the rest of the Pentateuch, most likely took place after the Exodus and before Israel's entrance into the land of Canaan, probably during the days of Israel's forty-year wilderness wandering. This author holds to an early date for the Exodus (about 1445 B.C.) and so assigns the date for the writing of Genesis at about 1425 B.C.

Purpose of Genesis

Genesis is the book of beginnings. It was written, first, to tell us clearly and definitely that God created all things directly. The entire organized universe was brought into existence by the powerful, all-knowing, creator God. Second, Genesis was written to record the beginning of many other elements that exist in our world today. The beginnings of such important matters as marriage, languages, nations, sin, and worship are recorded. A third purpose of the book is to relate how Israel,

Genesis

Important Data About Genesis

1. Key Word: Beginnings
2. Key Chapter: 12—The Abrahamic Covenant
3. Key Verses: 12:1–3
4. Key Characters: Adam, Eve, Noah, Abraham, Isaac, Jacob, Joseph
5. Meaning of "Genesis": A Greek word that means "origin" or "beginning"
6. Geography of Genesis: Ur, Canaan, Egypt

through Abraham, was selected from among the peoples of the world to become God's chosen nation.

Special Considerations on Genesis

Years Covered by Genesis

The total number of years covered in Genesis is uncertain because we do not know the time of creation. Genesis 12–50, from the call of Abraham to the death of Joseph, encompasses three hundred years. And we assign two thousand years to Genesis 1–11, so twenty-three hundred years is the estimate given for this book.

Background Points on Genesis

(a) The Nature of Genesis

It is historically accurate. The book of Genesis records actual human history. It is not a book of legends or religious myths. Adam, Eve, Noah, and the rest were real people whose lives and experiences are accurately recorded. The Lord Jesus Christ and the apostles and other writers of the Bible believed in the historicity of Genesis. Genesis is quoted some sixty times in the New Testament in seventeen different books (such as Matt. 24:37; Luke 11:51; Rom. 5:14; 1 Tim. 2:13). Genesis is scientifically accurate. Genesis records the origin of all created life and matter. It tells of a worldwide flood and numerous miracles. In all cases, Genesis speaks truthfully and accurately. Although it does not use modern scientific terminology, it speaks correctly. God is the source of all truth, whether it has to do with spiritual law or natural law.

Furthermore, Genesis is characterized by supernaturalism. The reader of Genesis is immediately confronted with the issue of supernaturalism as he opens to chapter 1. And in the rest of Genesis, God steps in on occasion and temporarily suspends natural law. This, of course, poses no problem to the believer who understands that God is personally involved with both His creation and His people.

(b) The Emphasis of Genesis

It is clear that the emphasis of Genesis is on God's covenant with Abraham and the initial outworking of that covenant relationship. The focus of thirty-nine chapters in Genesis is on four men—Abraham, Isaac, Jacob, and Joseph. By way of contrast, only two chapters are devoted to the creation of the entire universe, and only nine chapters are given over to man's earliest history. The first eleven chapters cover two thousand or more years, whereas the remaining thirty-nine chapters focus on three hundred years of history.

SUMMARY OF GENESIS

God's Dealings with Mankind in General (chaps. 1–11)

The Creation (1–2)

These two chapters affirm the fact of a special creation by God. Moses, in simple, nonscientific terms, states that God supernaturally created all things in the universe. He did not use any preexistent matter, but created the earth and the universe out of nothing (see Heb. 11:3). These two chapters answer the two key questions involving origins—the origin of the material universe and the origin of man. (For a discussion of the basic theories of origins, see "Various Views on Origins," page 30.)

The Days of Creation (1:1–31)

The opening statement in 1:1 is critical to our understanding of the creation account. This first verse summarizes the creation account to follow by declaring that God created the entire organized universe and everything in it ("heavens and earth"). The New Testament gives additional light by revealing that the Creator is the Triune God—Father, Son, and Holy Spirit (John 1:3; Col. 1:16 with Job 33:4; Ps. 33:6). The word used for "created" is the Hebrew word *bara,* which strongly supports the idea of the ex nihilo ("out of nothing") creation. Moses could have selected no better word than *bara* to express the idea of an extraordinary activity by God.[1] God simply called the universe into existence.

All of this activity took place "in the beginning," which refers to the creation week and not to billions of years in the past.

"'Beginning' refers to the commencement of time in our universe and demonstrates that the matter of the universe had a definite origin; it is not eternal and did not start itself."[2]

Furthermore, Exodus 20:11 and 31:17 help define the "beginning" by defining the chronological limits of creation as being within a six-day period.[3]

So with this simple but profound declaration, Moses states that there is a God, He is powerful, and He is greater than His creation.

Photograph of the eclipse of the sun. The creation of light marked a separation from darkness.

The implications of this first verse in the Old Testament are great. Since God is the one and only Creator, He has the power and the right to do what He chooses with His creation. He deserves to be honored and worshiped by His creatures (see Rev. 4:11). Unregenerate men, however, willfully resist acknowledging the great Creator God.

(a) Day 1: The creation of light (1:2–5)
God created the material earth on the first day (1:1). The earth had no distinct features such as mountains or continents, however. At this point it was unfinished and was uninhabited and empty ("formless and void").[4] It awaited God's creative activity.[5]

The creation of light was the next act of God, making a separation between darkness and light. God created a light source, which was not the sun, in order to temporarily mark off the day-night cycle, as the earth rotated on its axis. The sun was created on the fourth day, after the creation of the earth. Perhaps this was to speak out against the future pagan worship of the "creator" sun, the false religious science of astrology, and the evolutionary idea of the earth's coming from the sun.

Although there is no specific statement in Genesis 1 on the subject of angelic beings, they may have been created on the first day as part of the creation of the heavens and the earth (Ps. 148:2–5; Job 38:7).

(b) Day 2: The creation of the upper and lower waters (1:6–8)
By elevating some of the waters that were on the earth to a region above the earth, God created the earth's atmosphere. Some believe

that these upper waters were ordinary rain clouds.[6] Others believe that they formed a large vapor canopy that surrounded the earth, providing a "greenhouse" effect on the earth. This view also sees the upper waters as a great source of water for the Flood of Noah's day.[7]

(c) Day 3: The creation of plants (1:9–13)
God spoke and great areas of land suddenly appeared from beneath the lower waters. The earth, which had a cool crust, now had mountains, plains, and ocean basins. God then called trees and vegetation into existence. They were created full grown with the capacity to reproduce after their own kind.

(d) Day 4: The creation of the sun, moon, and stars (1:14–19)
Evidently the sun, moon, and stars were actually created on the fourth day and did not simply "appear." These luminaries were designed to give light to the earth and to function as a calendar for the earth, marking off days, months, years, and seasons. The sun and moon are "great lights" in the sense that this is the way they appear to those on the earth. It is the "language of appearance."

(e) Day 5: The creation of birds and all marine life (1:20–23)
All water creatures came into being on this day, leaving no room in the biblical text for evolution with its gradual development from single-celled, marine organisms.

(f) Day 6: The creation of land animals, reptiles, man (1:24–31)
After creating the animals, reptiles, and insects that would live on the earth, God turned His attention to the crown of creation, man. Only man would be created in the "image of God," which has reference to moral and spiritual likeness. Only man would be a "person," possessing intellect, emotions, and a will. Man was made to be "king of the earth" with authority to rule and to subdue the rest of creation.

When the creation week was completed, God's verdict was that it was all excellent (1:31).

The Creation of Man (2:1–25)
Genesis 2 is a further development of part of day six. It is simply giving greater attention to the creation of man. It is not, as some have suggested, a separate and different creation narrative.

(a) The Sabbath (2:1–3)
God set the seventh day apart, though there is no evidence that He commanded men to observe the Sabbath before the days of Moses (Ex. 16:23; 20:8–11; 31:12–17).

(b) Additional information (2:4–6)
This section probably refers to special types of vegetation that needed Adam's care.

(c) The creation of Adam (2:7–9)
Adam was created suddenly and supernaturally from the dust of the ground. After he was created, God placed him into the Garden of Eden. Also God placed two trees with special powers into the Garden—the tree of life and the tree of the knowledge of good and evil.

(d) The Garden of Eden (2:10–17)
Eden was a small area of the planet and would become the place where man's moral test would take place.

(e) The creation of Eve and the beginning of marriage (2:18–25)
Before Eve's creation, all Adam's relationships were vertical —to God above him and to the animals below him. Adam was "alone." In order to clarify this to Adam, God paraded the basic species of animals past Adam. Adam named them but in the process realized that he had no one as a "complement" to him. God gave Adam his needed helper by creating Eve. God did not create Eve from the dust of the ground, but from one of Adam's ribs to emphasize their oneness. Significant, foundational truths for marriage are found in this section.

The Fall of Man (3–5)
The Entrance of Sin (3:1–24)
The "very good" state of creation did not last for long. Satan, who may not have fallen very long before this, tempted Eve by casting doubt on the word of God and the goodness of God. She was deceived and took the fruit from the tree of the knowledge of good and evil (the experiential knowledge of moral good and evil). Adam was not deceived (1 Tim. 2:14) but nevertheless took of the fruit and sinned against God. This willful act brought about immediate spiritual death (Rom. 5:12–19) and many years later physical death. Adam and Eve were removed from Eden and faced a world cursed by God. And now God's great work of redemption had to begin.

An abundant pasture of flowers. God called trees and vegetation into existence.

Various Views on Origins

A variety of views has been proposed to answer the question of the origin of the earth and the universe. Great amounts of material have been written in defending and promoting various views. It is simply impossible to reproduce the argumentation of the various positions. A brief summary is given of these views, recognizing the fact that within each perspective there may be many different variations.

Evolution

The word *evolution* simply means "change," "development," or "progress." When applied to earth's origins it stands for the view that the world and that which is in it began and developed by means of natural processes. Starting with simple, single-celled organisms, new species of more complex and intricate forms have developed over a period of billions of years. Mutations, natural selection, and vast amounts of time are the basic elements of this view. A personal Creator God is not needed or wanted in this theory. For the Christian, this theory must be rejected.

Theistic Evolution

This view attempts to bring together the basic components of the theory of evolution with the Creator God of the Bible. The basic idea is that God created life but used the process of evolution to bring about the earth and the universe as we observe it today. This view holds that Adam's body was simply that of an animal that was the result of millions of years of evolutionary development. Several hundred thousand years ago, God placed an eternal soul into this apelike biped. This act is that which sets animals and man apart.

But in trying to combine these opposite views, "theistic evolution" has compromised the clear teaching of Scripture on such subjects as the direct creation of man, the nature of man, and the origin of sin and death. It has been careless with the words and text of Scripture.[8] This theory will be unacceptable to those who have a high view of Scripture and believe in careful exegesis.

Creationism

Creationism believes that almighty God supernaturally created the heavens and the earth by specific acts. Creation was out of nothing and was instantaneous. God did not use an evolutionary process to bring things into existence. Within creationism there are several basic viewpoints.

The Day-Age View

This view, also known as the Geologic Day View, generally holds that the days of creation in Genesis 1 were not literal twenty-four-hour days, but rather long periods of time. Thus, the earth is old, but man created

Charles Darwin, author of *The Origin of Species*, argued that life on earth evolved.

on the sixth day is relatively young. Some have held that the days of Genesis 1 are literal twenty-four-hour days, but that there are great amounts of time separating the days. This view is held by several authors.[9]

The Ruin-Reconstruction View

This view, also known as the Gap Theory, proposes a large gap in time between an original creation (found in Genesis 1:1) and a re-creation (found in Genesis 1:3–31). The basic idea is that in the dateless past, God created a heaven and an earth that were perfect. But then Satan fell into sin, and with him many other angelic beings also fell. Sin, therefore, entered the universe, and God destroyed the original earth, leaving it "waste and void." After vast amounts of time, God re-created the heavens and the earth. The days of Genesis 1 are literal twenty-four-hour days, but they describe the re-creation and not the original creation.[10]

The Literal Day View

This view holds that the days of creation in Genesis 1 are literal twenty-four-hour days and that they are the days of the original creation. The heavens and the earth that we observe today, though marred by sin, are those created in Genesis 1. This view also believes in a young earth (that the earth is tens of thousands of years old and not millions or billions).[11] The author of this book holds to this view.

The Basic Provisions of the Abrahamic Covenant

Personal Blessing for Abraham

God promised that Abraham would be the father of a great nation, have a multitude of descendants, and prosper materially (Gen. 12:2; 13:16; 15:5; 17:6). These promises to Abraham have been literally fulfilled.

Blessing to Abraham's Descendants

This aspect of the covenant does not apply to all of Abraham's physical descendants, but only to those who came through the line of Isaac and Jacob. This covenant was passed on from Abraham to Isaac only and then to Jacob (Gen. 26:3–6; 28:13–14; 35:9–12). As with Abraham, these descendants are promised greatness as a nation (Gen. 12:2; 13:16; 15:5). Also, they were guaranteed the land of Canaan as their own (Gen. 12:7; 13:15–17; 15:7–8; 17:8). The area was described generally in Genesis 15:18 as extending from the river of Egypt to the Euphrates River. More exact boundaries would be given later as Israel actually prepared to possess the land of promise. This aspect of the Abrahamic Covenant has not yet been fulfilled.

Universal Blessing

The covenant also looked beyond the line of Abraham to include all mankind: "And in you all the families of the earth shall be blessed" (Gen. 12:3). It was not God's intention to isolate Israel from the nations, but rather that Israel would be a worldwide blessing (Gen. 18:18; 22:17–18; 26:3–4; 28:13–14). The ultimate fulfillment of this part of the covenant will be in "the seed" of Abraham, the Lord Jesus Christ (Gal. 3:16). This aspect of the covenant has been, is being, and will be fulfilled.

The Nature of the Abrahamic Covenant

It Is an Everlasting Covenant

Several times God declared that this covenant was to be everlasting (Gen. 13:15; 17:7–8,13,19). No time limit was placed on this covenant relationship. Israel was to remain a nation forever and would remain in their relationship with the Lord (Jer. 31:36).

It Is an Unconditional Covenant

Nearly all covenants made between men or nations were conditional in character; that is, certain conditions had to be fulfilled by one participant in the covenant before the other participant was obligated to do his part. For example, in the Mosaic Covenant God promised to bless Israel, if she obeyed His commandments.

The Abrahamic Covenant, however, was unconditional. God committed Himself to do certain things for Abraham and the nation that would come from him. Failure or unbelief on Abraham's or Israel's part would not set aside this covenant. This is an extremely critical point in interpreting numerous passages of Scripture that have to do with Israel's possession of the land of Canaan, her continuance as a nation, the reign of her Messiah on the earth, and her future redemption. The unconditional character of this covenant is undoubtedly one of the most important keys in Bible interpretation.

One view is that the Abrahamic Covenant had no conditions attached to it except the original one, that Abraham must leave his homeland of Ur of the Chaldees and go to the land of Canaan. Once he did that the covenant was unconditional.

> It is important to observe the relation of obedience to this covenant program. Whether God would institute a covenant program with Abraham or not depended upon Abraham's act of obedience in leaving the land. When once this act was accomplished, and Abraham did obey God, God instituted an irrevocable, unconditional program.[12]

> Except for the original condition of leaving his homeland and going to the promised land, the covenant is made with no conditions whatever. It is rather a prophetic declaration of God of what will certainly come to pass, and is no more conditional than any other announced plan of God which depends upon God's sovereignty for its fulfillment.[13]

This position properly emphasizes the unconditional nature of the Abrahamic Covenant and puts one on solid ground for interpreting the rest of the Old Testament. Another view that also correctly underscores the unconditional character of the covenant states that the word from God to Abraham, "Go forth from your country" (Gen. 12:1), is not a condition, but is rather an invitation.

> This imperative is followed by two imperfects and then a series of cohortative imperfects in verses 2–3. But does a command amount to a formal condition on the divine intention to bless? . . . the accent of the passage was on the cohortatives which emphasized intentionality rather than obligation. . . . The summons to "go," then, was an invitation to receive the gift of promise by faith.[14]

This position suggests that there was not an "original" condition to the Abrahamic Covenant. In either view, the proper emphasis is on the unconditionality of the covenant.

As the Abrahamic Covenant was repeated and enlarged, there were no conditions attached to it. After repeating

The Abrahamic Covenant

The idea of a covenant between individuals was dominant in the life of the ancient Near East. It is often seen in the Old Testament. Covenants made between men (e.g., Gen. 21:32), between groups (e.g., 1 Sam. 11:1), and between nations (e.g., Ex. 23:32) were common. A covenant was an agreement between two parties that bound them together with common interests and responsibilities. It was most serious and sacred to enter into a covenant. And covenants usually included blessings and cursings—blessings upon the one who fulfilled his part in the covenant and cursings on the one who broke his oath.

When God made a covenant with Abraham, therefore, it was not a strange or unusual event. Granted, one did not usually enter into a covenant with the almighty God. But Abraham would be thoroughly familiar with the idea of a covenant and the making of a covenant. The record of the covenant made with Abraham is found in Genesis 12:1–3; 13:14–17; 15:1–21; 17:1–22; and 22:15–18.

the promise to Abraham in Genesis 13, God confirms His promise in Genesis 15, when He alone passes between the pieces of the sacrificial animals. Later (Gen. 17), God commanded that circumcision be part of the covenant—not as a condition, but rather as a "sign." When the covenant was confirmed to Isaac and then to Jacob, no conditions were attached. As time went on, even when Israel was unfaithful to the covenant, God remained faithful (Jer. 31:36). The writers of the New Testament also saw the covenant as based on God's promises and not subject to change (Heb. 6:13–18; Gal. 3:15–18).

One additional point must be made. The eventual complete fulfillment of the Abrahamic Covenant depended on God, and not on Abraham, Isaac, Jacob, or the nation of Israel. But the sins of these men and the unbelief of Israel did have significance. Although their failure would never negate the covenant, it would affect their own blessing and could even temporarily hinder the program of God.[15] Examples of such failures and their consequences are found scattered throughout the Old Testament. So even though the Abrahamic Covenant had no conditions attached to it, unbelief on the part of its recipients could, and often did, remove them from the place of favor and blessing. They would be "a mere transmitter of the blessing without personally inheriting any of its gifts directly."[16]

The Abrahamic Covenant and the Other Biblical Covenants

The first three covenants given below are enlargements of the Abrahamic Covenant, and, as such, are also eternal and unconditional. These "subcovenants" further define the provisions originally given to Abraham.

The Palestinian (Land) Covenant

This covenant focused on Israel's right to the land of Canaan. God had promised Abraham that the land was his "forever" (Gen. 13:15; 17:8). The Palestinian Covenant confirmed that the title deed did belong to Israel. But it also made clear that even though they owned the land, they could be removed from it because of sin. The covenant also promised that, in the future, Israel would be converted and restored permanently to the land. (See Deut. 30:4–10; Lev. 26:14, 32–42; Num. 34:1–12; Ezek. 36:24–36.)

The Davidic Covenant

This covenant develops the original promises having to do with dynasty, nation, and throne. The promises of the seed of Abraham were developed in the Davidic Covenant. (See 2 Sam. 7:11–16; Ps. 89:3–36; Jer. 33:14–22.)

The New Covenant

This covenant focuses on the spiritual blessing and redemption of Israel. It goes beyond Israel, however, and includes the Gentiles as well: "And in you all the families of the earth shall be blessed" (Gen. 12:3). (See Jer. 31:31–40; Luke 22:20; Heb. 8:6–13.)

The Mosaic Covenant

This is a conditional covenant made between God and Israel at Mount Sinai. It is not a part of the Abrahamic Covenant. It was a conditional covenant and was designed to be temporary.

The Story of Cain and Abel (4:1–25)
The effect of sin was seen early in the human experience as Cain murdered his brother Abel, and an apparent division between the godly and the ungodly appeared.

The Descendants of Adam (5:1–32)
Genesis 5 is given to take us quickly from the days of Adam to the times of Noah. This chapter also shows the fulfillment of the curse (2:17) of death on man because of sin.

The Flood (6–9)
The Catastrophe (6:1–8:19)
By the days of Noah, mankind had degenerated completely, and the world had become a terrible place to live (Gen. 6:5, 11, 13). Sin had gripped man so completely that only Noah was said to be righteous (Gen. 6:9; Heb. 11:7). God declared that He would destroy the world with a flood of water (6:17). Noah was ordered to build an ark to save all air-breathing creatures. This bargelike structure was about 450 feet long, 75 feet wide, and 45 feet high. It had three decks, giving it about 95,700 square feet of space.[17] It had plenty of room to handle its live cargo.

The Flood that came 120 years after God's pronouncement of judgment on mankind was universal. This is seen in the use of global terms such as "all" and "every" in describing the destruction of those days. The fact that the Flood lasted for more than a year (something not true of local floods) indicates that Noah's Flood engulfed the whole earth. Furthermore, the statement of Genesis that all the high mountains were covered by more than twenty feet of water dictates a flood that is not confined to a local area (7:19–20). Even the building of an ark at all and the gathering of animals to it makes little sense unless the Flood was worldwide.[18] Psalm 104:1–9 speaks of worldwide, catastrophic geologic activity during the time of the Flood.[19] All of these factors point to the Flood as a supernatural judgment of universal scope.

Noah and His Family (8:20–9:28)
The Flood did not solve man's sin problem, though it did deal with a crisis of wickedness and reveal the power, holiness, and grace of God. When Noah and his family departed from the ark, a new era began, and God gave them some new guidelines. Commonly referred to

Plan of the Ark, showing its immense size in comparison with a modern building and truck.

Three decks | Skylight | Roof | Length: 450 feet (137 meters)

Artist's reconstruction of a Sumerian ziggurat, possibly similar to the biblical Tower of Babel.

as the "Noahic covenant," these guidelines included the following: man was to spread out over the whole earth; man could now eat meat; man had the right to execute murderers; and man would now be instinctively feared by animals (9:1–7). God promised He would never again destroy the world by water, and He gave the rainbow as a sign of this covenant (9:12–15).

The Nations (10–11)

The Ancient Families (10:1–32)

This chapter is a partial record of the development of the human race through the sons of Noah. There is an emphasis on the Canaanites and their land, since Moses wanted to link all this information to God's promise to bless Israel as a nation in the Promised Land of Canaan.[20] The family of Shem is mentioned

Great door

The ark was longer than a dozen big school buses or two dozen family cars, and taller than a four-story school building.

Height: 45 feet (14 meters)
Width: 75 feet (23 meters)

last in the account because the rest of the Old Testament is the story of Abraham, a descendant of Shem.

The Tower of Babel (11:1–32)

The incident at the Tower of Babel explains how the human race became so divided when it had all descended from one man and his family. Chapter 11 chronologically precedes chapter 10. In spite of God's command to spread out over the earth (9:1–7), man chose to disobey and to congregate together (11:4). Foreseeing the resulting wickedness, God intervened with a unique act of judgment. He brought total chaos and confusion to man by causing the people at Babel ("confusion") to begin speaking separate and distinct languages. The result was a dispersion of the human race to separate geographic areas.[21] This event marks the origin of the different human languages and, perhaps, the beginning of distinct racial groups.

The chapter ends (11:10–32) by listing the generations of Shem leading up to Abraham. Some two thousand years of the early history of man have been sketched, and now Moses is ready to record the call of Abraham. With Abraham's call, the second major division of the Old Testament is opened.

God's Dealings with the Nation of Israel (chaps. 12–50)

Abraham (12–23)

The Call of Abraham (12:1–9)

These verses record the second call of Abraham (Abram). God first called Abraham when he lived in Ur of the Chaldees (Gen. 11:31; Acts 7:2–4) Abraham and several family members departed Ur and traveled to Haran, which was located in the northern part of the Fertile Crescent. After several years there and after the death of Terah, his father, Abraham left Haran. He evidently did not know exactly where God was leading him (Heb. 11:8) but knew enough to head for Canaan. God confirmed His covenant when Abraham arrived in Canaan at the age of seventy-five. This covenant is the cornerstone of the Old Testament. Without an understanding of the Abrahamic Covenant, there will be little understanding of the purposes and plans of God.

The Testings of Abraham (12:10–15:21)

After God confirmed the covenant with him in Canaan, Abraham traveled around the southern part of the land. (Archaeology reveals that southern Canaan was sparsely populated at this time, allowing Abraham the opportunity to move about freely.) Abraham built altars wherever he went, showing his awareness of the presence of God.

Before much time had elapsed a severe famine hit Canaan, and Abraham went to Egypt. It was evidently a time of failure in the life of this patriarch. (A "patriarch" was the legal and spiritual head of the family. He had great power over his clan, but also was responsible for the well-being and protection of all in his family unit.) Abraham did not evidence faith in the Lord when he fled to Egypt, nor when he had Sarah, his wife, lie about their relationship (12:10–20).

Returning from Egypt, Abraham separated himself from his nephew Lot, renewed his faith in the Lord at Bethel, and experienced

God's Covenants with Israel

The Chronology of the Patriarchs

This chronology is based upon some key verses that assign specific lengths of time between important Old Testament events. These verses are 1 Kings 6:1 and Exodus 12:40. If these verses are taken at face value, then the list given below is relatively accurate.

	Date B.C.	Age of the Patriarch	Scripture in Genesis	Event in Genesis
A	2165	–	11:26	Abraham born in Ur
B	2090	75	12:4	Abraham enters Canaan
R	2079	86	16:5	Ishmael born to Hagar
A	2065	100	21:2	Isaac born to Sarah
H	2050	115	22:6	Isaac taken to Mt. Moriah
A	2028	137	23:1	Sarah dies at age 127
M	2025	140	25:20	Abraham sees Isaac married
	1990	175	25:7	The death of Abraham
I	2065	–	21:2	Isaac born to Sarah
S	2025	40	25:20	Isaac marries Rebekah
A	2005	60	25:24	Esau and Jacob born to Isaac
A	1928	137	27:1	Isaac deceived by Jacob
C	1885	180	35:28	The death of Isaac
	2005	–	25:24	Jacob born to Isaac
J	1928	77	28:2	Jacob steals the blessing
A	1921	84	29:32	Reuben born–Jacob's first
C	1908	97	35:1	Jacob returns to Bethel
O	1875	130	46:5	Jacob moves to Egypt with family
B	1858	147	47:28	The death of Jacob
J	1914	–	30:22	Joseph born to Rachel
O	1897	17	37:2	Joseph sold by his brothers
S	1884	30	41:46	Joseph made second ruler in Egypt
E	1858	56	47:28	Blessing given—Jacob dies
P	1804	110	50:26	The death of Joseph
H				

some food. Because of this act, Esau not only lost his birthright but is called a "profane" person by the Scriptures (Heb. 12:16). Evidently Esau assumed that since he was the favorite of his father, Isaac, he would receive all the possessions and favors he wanted when his father gave the "blessing." He was probably correct in his thinking. However, Jacob deceived Isaac and took the blessing for himself (Gen. 27:1–45).

Abraham's drama of sacrifice of Isaac took place on Mount Moriah, where two thousand years later God would sacrifice His Son, Jesus, for the sins of the world.

In an essentially nonliterate society, oral transactions were extremely important; and the oral blessing had the force of a legally-binding oral will, as texts from the Mesopotamian city of Nuzi demonstrate. The binding character of the blessing is clear because Esau did not argue for a transfer of the blessing to him just because a mistake had been made. He merely asked for some additional blessing.[29]

In order to avoid the wrath of his brother, Esau, Jacob fled to Haran to the house of his uncle, Laban. Here Jacob stayed for twenty years. Through a series of schemes and circumstances, Jacob accumulated a great deal of wealth as well as two wives, two concubines, and eleven sons (28:1–31:55). When Jacob returned to Canaan, after the twenty years in Haran, a twelfth son was born to him. These twelve sons of Jacob were to become the foundation stones of the nation that God was building.

Jacob was known for his scheming and deceit. But upon his return to Canaan, he met the Lord in a unique way (32:1–32). After this encounter he was a different man, transformed by God. Jacob (meaning "supplanter") had his name changed to Israel (meaning "having power with God").

Jacob settled in southern Canaan, and the story of God's making a "great nation" continued with the focus shifting away from Jacob to Joseph, his eleventh son.

Abraham's Family Tree

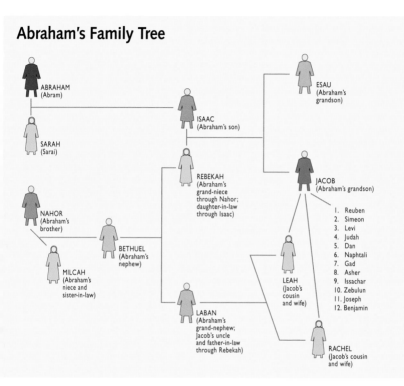

ABRAHAM
(Abram)

SARAH
(Sarai)

NAHOR
(Abraham's
brother)

MILCAH
(Abraham's
niece and
sister-in-law)

BETHUEL
(Abraham's
nephew)

ISAAC
(Abraham's son)

REBEKAH
(Abraham's
grand-niece
through Nahor;
daughter-in-law
through Isaac)

LABAN
(Abraham's
grand-nephew;
Jacob's uncle
and father-in-law
through Rebekah)

ESAU
(Abraham's
grandson)

JACOB
(Abraham's grandson)

1. Reuben
2. Simeon
3. Levi
4. Judah
5. Dan
6. Naphtali
7. Gad
8. Asher
9. Issachar
10. Zebulun
11. Joseph
12. Benjamin

LEAH
(Jacob's
cousin
and wife)

RACHEL
(Jacob's cousin
and wife)

Joseph (37–50)

Jacob made the fundamental mistake of openly showing favoritism toward Joseph. This generated the envy and hatred of Joseph's older brothers. They plotted to kill Joseph, but later changed their minds and sold their seventeen-year-old brother to a caravan that was headed for Egypt. The brothers then deceived their father, Jacob, into believing that Joseph had been killed by wild animals.

Through an amazing set of circumstances that were directed by the Lord, Joseph (now thirty years old, 41:46) became the second most powerful ruler in the land of Egypt. All this was part of God's plan for preserving His nation.

A severe famine hit Egypt and Canaan, forcing the sons of Jacob to leave Canaan and come to Egypt to buy food that was available there. After discovering that his brothers had changed, Joseph revealed himself to his amazed brothers. What followed was a grand

Locations in Genesis

A. The four Patriarchs

Abraham	11:26, 29: 12–25
Isaac	17:19; 21:3; 22:2; 24:62; 27; 35:28
Jacob	25:26; 27–35; 42–49
Joseph	30:24; 37–50

B. Wives and Children of the Patriarchs

12 Sons	29:31–35; 30:5–13; 30:17–24; 35:16
Dinah	34
Esau	25:25; 26:34; 27; 33:4; 36:1
Hagar	16:1; 21:14
Ishmael	16:11–15; 17:20; 21:9; 25:9–12
Keturah	25:1–6
Leah	29:16
Rachel	29:6–16; 35:16
Rebekah	22:23; 24:15
Sarah	11:29; 16:1; 17:15; 18:9; 20:12; 21:3; 23:2

C. Other Relatives in the Family Tree

Bethuel	22:23; 24:15, 50
Haran	11:26–28
Laban	24:29; 28:5
Lot	11:26; 12:4; 13:5; 14:12; 19:1
Milcah	11:29; 22:20
Nahor	11:26–29; 22:20
Terah	11:26, 31

family reunion in Egypt. Jacob and all the other members of the family came to live in Egypt, under the protective care of Joseph. The "nation" now had a population of about seventy-five (46:27).

Egypt now became the protector of the infant nation. God was placing His baby nation into the incubator of Egypt until it was grown up enough to fend for itself. Egypt protected Israel in three ways. First, it protected Israel physically. Although the Egyptian army was unaware of it, they were guarding Israel against countless kings and robber bands that could have wiped out this young nation in a matter of hours. Second, Egypt shielded Israel morally. Although Egypt may not have been known for its righteousness, it was superior to the wicked Canaanites. By removing Israel from the degrading influence of these perverse Canaanite people, God was preserving His people from moral failure, which surely would have come if they had been left in Canaan. Third, Egypt secured Israel's racial purity. Israel would certainly have intermarried with the Canaanites (as Genesis 34 reveals), but they would not intermarry with the Egyptians. The Egyptians looked down on the Israelites because of their occupation of shepherding (46:34), and this was a key factor in keeping these two peoples apart.

Genesis ends with Israel safely inside the protective boundaries of Egypt. The nation has no land, no law, and only seventy-five people. But God is at work, and He will bring to pass His promise to Abraham, "And I will make you a great nation."

The Mosaic Authorship of the Pentateuch

For well over one hundred years there has been a debate on the authorship of the Pentateuch. Conservative scholars have consistently affirmed that Moses wrote it, whereas liberal scholars have denied Mosaic authorship.

Those who deny the Mosaic authorship of the Pentateuch today basically build their view on the theories of Jean Astruc (an eighteenth-century French writer) and Julius Wellhausen (a nineteenth-century liberal German theologian). Those who deny Mosaic authorship hold to the "documentary hypothesis" (known also as the JEDP Theory). This theory maintains that the Pentateuch was composed from a number of documents. These documents actually were written many centuries after the time of Moses, and Moses had nothing to do with their composition. His name was simply attached to them to give them greater value and acceptance. Some who held this theory declared that Moses could not have written the Pentateuch since he could not write, assuming that writing was not a part of life in the times of Moses. Since Wellhausen's day, however, archaeological finds have totally debunked this idea, showing that writing and literary interests were very much a part of life in Egypt and elsewhere in the ancient near east fifteen hundred years before the days of Moses.[30]

Liberal scholars teach that the documents were actually written between 850 and 500 B.C. At that time, some unknown man (or men) known as a redactor, then put these documents together in the order and arrangement of our Pentateuch. These various documents were known by the letters JEDP.

J represented the document composed by the school of writers who preferred the Divine name Jehovah, E the writers preferring Elohim, D the writer of the Book of Deuteronomy, and P the writer of those sections of the Pentateuch having to do especially with priestly liturgy, sacrifice, and genealogical and chronological sections.[31]

This "documentary hypothesis" has been effectively answered by conservative scholars. They have pointed out not only the basic invalidity of the major points of the theory and the evolutionary philosophy behind the theory, but also the terrible bias against the supernatural nature of the Scriptures.[32]

Several lines of evidence support the

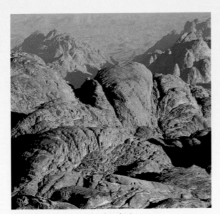

View from Mount Sinai, Jebel Musa.

Mosaic authorship of the Pentateuch. First, the Pentateuch itself claims that Moses wrote many important parts (Ex. 17:14; 24:4; 34:27; Lev. 1:1; 4:1; 6:1, 8; Num. 1:1, 19; 33:2; Deut. 1:1; 17:18; 31:9, 24–26). Second, other Old Testament books declare that Moses wrote the Pentateuch (e.g., Josh. 1:7–8; 8:31–34; 22:5; 1 Kings 2:3; 2 Chron. 23:18; 34:14; Dan. 9:11, 13; Ezra 3:2; Neh. 8:1; 13:1–3). Third, Christ believed that Moses wrote the first five books of the Old Testament. The Lord Jesus spoke of certain truths that Moses wrote or spoke of the Old Testament scriptures in terms as "Moses and the prophets" and "Moses, the Psalms and the prophets" (Matt. 8:4; 19:7–8; Mark 7:10; 12:26; Luke 16:29, 31; 24:44; John 1:45; 5:46; 7:19). Fourth, the writers of the New Testament attribute the Pentateuch to Moses (Acts 3:22; 26:22; 28:23; Rom. 10:5, 19). Fifth, the testimony of tradition has been unanimous in support of Mosaic authorship. Literature from the intertestamental period, from the early church, and from the church of later centuries have agreed on Moses as the writer of Genesis through Deuteronomy. Only recently has there been an unfounded challenge to Mosaic authorship by liberal critics.

It should be noted that the Pentateuch is fully inspired by God. But the truth of inspiration does not eliminate a variety of sources being used by Moses. (Luke used a number of different sources in putting his gospel together according to Luke 1:1–4.) Moses received some information directly from God (e.g., the law at Mount Sinai). Some truth was written down because Moses himself was an eyewitness of some events (e.g., the plagues on Egypt and the wilderness wanderings). Other information may have come from very ordinary means such as written documents or oral tradition (e.g., the account of the Flood of Noah or the many stories of the patriarchs). Inspiration has to do with the accurate recording of the truth. God guided this man Moses, using Moses' personality, vocabulary, and experiences, keeping him from error of any kind. "Inspiration argues only for accuracy of the written record; it does not stipulate that the writer had a mind that functioned as a blank tablet to be written on by the Holy Spirit."[33]

The Pentateuch, therefore, is an inspired, inerrant, authoritative document written by the man Moses.

4.

Exodus &
Leviticus

EXODUS

INTRODUCTION TO EXODUS

Authorship and Date of Exodus

Moses wrote the book of Exodus as well as the other books of the Pentateuch. Since Exodus is a record of Israel's departure from Egypt (about 1445 B.C.), this book was most likely written about 1425 B.C. (For a further discussion of the date of Israel's exodus out of Egypt, see "The Date of the Exodus," page 60.)

Purpose of Exodus

Exodus continues the story of God's dealings with the descendants of Abraham. It picks up

---

Exodus

The Chronology of Genesis and Exodus

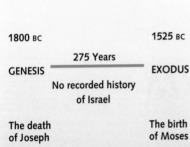

1800 BC   1525 BC

275 Years

GENESIS   EXODUS

No recorded history of Israel

The death of Joseph   The birth of Moses

Important Data About Exodus

1. Key Word: Redemption
2. Key Chapters: 12—The "exodus" out of Egypt; 20—The giving of the law
3. Key Verses: 3:7–8; 15:13
4. Key Characters: Moses, Aaron, Joshua, and Pharaoh
5. Meaning of "Exodus": A Greek word that means "exit" or "departure"
6. Geography of Exodus: Egypt, the wilderness, Mount Sinai

the history of the people of Israel after a silent period of 275 years. During this lengthy period two significant things happened. First, Israel's population, which was about seventy-five at the end of Genesis, grew to about 2.5 million. And second, the people of Israel became enslaved to the Egyptians.

Exodus also records the giving of the law at Mount Sinai. The "constitution" given to Israel marks the second significant step in the process of becoming God's great nation. But before Israel could receive her new law code, God had to redeem His slave people out of the bondage of Egypt with a display of awesome power.

Special Considerations on Exodus

Years Covered by Exodus
Technically the book of Exodus covers about eighty years, from the birth of Moses to the arrival of Israel at Mount Sinai. The emphasis of the book, however, is on the two-year period of Israel's departure from Egypt.

Background Points on Exodus
(a) The Importance of Exodus
Practically every book in the Old Testament makes some reference back to this book, referring to the Exodus, the mighty miracles of God in the release of His people from slavery.

The Chronology of the Life of Moses

1525	1485	1445	1405
MOSES IN PHARAOH'S COURT	MOSES IN EXILE IN MIDIAN	MOSES WITH ISRAEL IN THE WILDERNESS	
40 Years	40 Years	40 Years	

or the law that was given at Mount Sinai. This book is also important historically. It records those early days of Israel as a fledgling nation, the receiving of its constitution and the origins of many religious customs and practices of Israel. Exodus has importance spiritually because there is much in the experiences of Israel that corresponds to our own Christian lives. Many principles of the spiritual life are played out in the successes and failures of the nation.

(b) Some Important Background Scriptures

In Genesis 15:13–14, the enslavement and residence in Egypt was foretold. These years in Egypt were all part of God's purposes for Israel, and they did not catch God off guard. Genesis 50:24–26 records the last words of Joseph and his testimony to God's future deliverance. The bones of Joseph evidently became a visible reminder that God was going to fulfill His promises (see Ex. 13:19 and Heb. 11:22). Stephen's sermon in Acts 7:20–36 and the record found in Hebrews 11:23–29 give some insights and analysis not found in Exodus itself.

SUMMARY OF EXODUS

The Journey from Egypt to Mount Sinai (chaps. 1–18)

Events Leading Up to the Exodus from Egypt (1–14)

Israel in Egyptian Bondage (1:1–6:30)
The historical silence of 275 years is broken in chapter 1 when Moses relates two important facts. First, the nation experienced a tremen-dous growth (1:7), and second, the nation fell out of favor with the rulers and into slavery (1:8–11). There is much debate over who these oppressors of Israel were. Some argue persuasively that those who put Israel into slavery were a largely Semitic people known as the Hyksos,[1] whereas others present strong evidence that the oppressors were native Egyptians.[2] Whichever group it was, Israel became the target of oppression and brutality. It was into that setting of slavery that God's deliverer Moses was born (2:1–9). Through some God-directed circumstances, Moses spent the first forty years of his life enjoying the palace life of Egypt (2:11 with Acts 7:23). But because of his own impulsive, violent actions Moses was forced to escape from Egypt to the land of Midian, where he spent the next forty years of his life tending flocks (2:11–22).

When Moses was eighty years old (7:7), God's time for redeeming His people out of slavery came. God "remembered" His covenant with Abraham (2:24) and called Moses to be His man to confront Pharaoh, king of Egypt. Though Moses was reluctant to be the leader and gave numerous objections to God (see 3:11; 3:13; 4:1; 4:10; 4:13), he nevertheless was used mightily by God in delivering Israel. Since Pharaoh was not willing to release Israel, God employed a series of miraculous plagues on Egypt to accomplish His purposes.

The Plagues of God on Egypt (7:1–11:10)
When confronted by Moses to release Israel, Pharaoh arrogantly challenged God (5:2). The ten plagues that followed and the incident at the Red Sea answered that challenge and educated Pharaoh on the subject of "who is the

The haunting image of the sphinx, Cairo, Egypt.

Lord?" But these miraculous deeds also instructed the people of Israel (8:22).

The plagues were essentially a contest between the true and living God of Israel and the whole multitude of false gods that were the objects of Egyptian worship (Ex. 12:12; Num. 33:4). Although God used natural phenomena, such as hail and frogs, these plagues were still supernatural. The supernatural character of the plagues is seen in that they were predicted ahead of time, they were extraordinarily intense, and they discriminated between Israel and Egypt (from the fourth plague onward). The plagues, which may have lasted about nine months from start to finish, devastated both the people and the land of Egypt (see Ps. 78:44–51; 105:26–38). With the climactic, ter-

rible plague of the death of the firstborn (11:1–5), God broke the grip of the oppressors and led His people out of slavery.

The Institution of the Passover (12:1–13:16)

God gave to Israel a new calendar based on this meaningful event. The Passover sacrifice beautifully pictured the Lord Jesus Christ, our Passover (1 Cor. 5:7). Israel had to use a lamb that was in the prime of life and had no blemish (John 1:29; Acts 2:22, 27). The perfect lamb had to be slain, the blood shed (Heb. 9:28), and the blood applied (John 3:36). Doing these things would save a person from judgment (John 5:24). As a result of the Passover, all the firstborn in Israel now belonged to the Lord (13:1–16; Num. 3:44–45).

The Destruction of the Egyptian Army (13:17–14:31)

When Pharaoh saw that the Israelites had actually left the land, his hardened, sinful heart drove him to go after them. Trapped between the Red Sea and the oncoming Egyptian army, Israel seemed doomed. But God performed one of the great miracles of the Old Testament by parting the waters of the Red Sea and allowing His people to escape. God then destroyed the Egyptian army, which had ventured in after Israel (14:21–31). Deliverance was complete.

The Journey to Mount Sinai (15–18)

The spectacular and timely deliverance at the Red Sea brought forth praise from the lips of Moses and the people (15:1–21). But after only

The Plagues in Egypt

Scripture	Plague	Israel exempt?	Egyptian gods involved
1. 7:14–25	Nile River to blood	No	Hapi—spirit of the Nile Khnum—guardian of the Nile
2. 8.1–15	Frogs	No	Heqt—form of a frog Hapi—spirit of Nile
3. 8:16–19	Swarms of lice/gnats	No	Uncertain; perhaps attack on Egyptian priests
4. 8:20–32	Flies	Yes	Uatchit—a god who manifested himself as a fly
5. 9:17	Disease on the cattle	Yes	Apis bull revered. Sacred bulls and cows. Plah, Mnevis, Hathor
6. 9:8–11	Boils/sores on man and animal	Yes	Sekhmet—goddess with power to heal. Serapis—healing god
7. 9:12–35	Destruction of crops and cattle by hail	Yes	Seth—protector of crops Nut—sky goddess
8. 10:1–20	Destruction of crops by locust	Yes	Isis—goddess of life Seth—protector of crops
9. 10:21–29	Darkness	Yes	Re—sun god. Atum—god of setting sun. Amon-Re.
10. 11:1–10	Death of firstborn	Yes—if blood properly applied	Osiris—giver of life Pharaoh also was considered deity

three days into the journey Israel began to grumble about their situation; in this case the lack of water. This was the first of many times Israel would complain.

The journey to Mount Sinai took about three months. Moses recorded four places where Israel stopped along the way. At Marah (15:22–26), bitter waters were miraculously made drinkable. At the oasis of Elim they rested (15:27). Next, Israel journeyed into the Wilderness of Sin (16:1–36) where God met their need for food by supernaturally supplying manna (16:31). This supplying of manna for food on a daily basis would last for forty years. Rephidim was the fourth stop recorded by Moses. It was here that God met the need for water by bringing water from out of a rock. Also at Rephidim, Joshua is mentioned for the first time as he led the people of Israel in their first military battle as a nation, a victory over the army of the Amalekites. God proved again and again during the three-month trek to Mount Sinai that He would care for His people.

The Giving of the Law at Mount Sinai (chaps. 19–40)

The Preparation for the Giving of the Law (19–25)

The area around Mount Sinai was familiar to Moses. It was there that he had been caring for his flock when God confronted him at the burning bush (3:1–6). Mount Sinai (or Horeb, as it is also called, Ex. 3:1; 19:11; Deut. 4:10) was to be the place where Israel would meet God and receive the law (3:12). But before the law was actually given, Israel had to commit herself to obeying it (19:5–8). Four different times in chapter 19, Moses went up and down the mountain, communicating God's words to the people and the people's words to God (19:3, 8, 20, 24). Once the people agreed to this conditional covenant (19:8), and once they cleansed themselves (19:10), God came down upon the mountain to give them some of their "constitution." He demonstrated great power in order that the people might fear Him and understand the seriousness of their commitment (see Ex. 19:16; 20:20; Heb. 12:18).

The Giving of the Ten Commandments (20)

Before one law was given, God made clear that He had the right to regulate Israel's living since He was the One who had delivered her out of slavery (20:2).

The Ten Commandments do not constitute the whole of the law. These ten laws reflect spiritual and moral principles upon which the hundreds of laws in the Mosaic law code rest. There are more than six hundred other laws in Israel's constitution. The first four of the Ten Commandments stress man's relationship to God, and the last six emphasize man's relationship to man. These laws revealed God's holiness and the resulting standards for His people.

The Giving of the Civil Laws (21–24)

These laws revealed God's great concern about the details of life; that nothing was outside of His interest and involvement. Included in this section are laws governing slavery (21:1–11); personal injury laws (21:12–36); property laws (22:1–15); morality, finances, and offerings (22:16–21); laws covering civil obligations (23:1–19); and ceremonial laws (23:10–19). These laws do not give a complete ethical code; that is, not every possible circumstance or issue was dealt with. These laws did, however, give examples from which application to life situations was to be made. Later on, God would establish the priests to settle disputes by interpreting and applying the law (Deut. 17:8–13).

The Tabernacle and Its Service (25–40)
Preparing for Construction of the Tabernacle (25:1–31:18)

Two important events were to take place at Mount Sinai. First was the giving of the law, and second was the building of the Tabernacle. The Tabernacle was the portable worship center of Israel. Here Israel would be able to come to sacrifice and worship and have fellowship with God. Later, when Israel lived permanently in their land, the Tabernacle would be replaced by the Temple, a permanent structure in the city of Jerusalem. But for about 450 years the Tabernacle would be the central place for

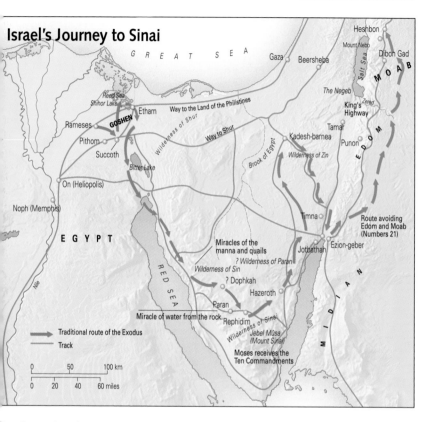

Israel's Journey to Sinai

Traditional route of the Exodus
Track

Israel's worship of the Lord.

At Mount Sinai, the detailed Tabernacle plans were given to Moses (25:40). The Tabernacle was to be surrounded with an outer court. The Tabernacle itself (the tentlike structure) would have two areas: the holy place and the holy of holies. Several altars and pieces of furniture were part of the plan. The Tabernacle had to be built just right, down to the last detail, because it was a picture of the person and redemptive work of Jesus Christ (Heb. 9:8–12).

The Incident of the Golden Calf
(32:1–34:35)

One of the greatest problems Israel would deal with in the days ahead was idolatry. The first two of the Ten Commandments warned

Artist's impression of the Tabernacle. It is not clear whether the Tabernacle had a pitched or flat roof.

against it. Yet, when Moses went up on the mountain for about six weeks, leaving his brother Aaron in charge (24:14), the law was quickly forgotten. In spite of the law and in spite of the awesome power of the Lord God in His total conquest of the gods of Egypt, Israel fell quickly into idolatry and the immorality that accompanied it. Aaron made a golden calf, and the people worshiped it. When Moses came down off the mountain, he disciplined the people for God and interceded with God for the people. Thousands died because of this event (32:28), and the matter was soon settled. But the incident was an ominous indicator of what lay ahead for the nation.

The Construction of the Tabernacle (35:1–40:38)
The construction of the Tabernacle was to be financed by a freewill offering from the people (25:2; 36:5–7). More than enough was received, and the materials were given to two men, Bezalel and Oholiab (31:2–6), who were to actually put the Tabernacle together. These men were blessed with great skill and wisdom from God. When the Tabernacle and its furnishings were complete, the glory of God filled the structure. God had taken up residence among His people (40:34–38). Now that the Tabernacle was built and the law was given, it was time to leave Mount Sinai and journey to Canaan, the land of promise. The nation had people, and they now had their constitution. Only the possessing of the land remained to make them a great nation. (For further discussion of God's revelation of Himself to Israel, see "The Names of God in the Old Testament," page 42.)

LEVITICUS

The book of Leviticus complements Exodus; it does not advance the story of the Old Testament, although there is a brief historical portion in it (chaps. 8–10). Along with Exodus, Leviticus records the law code of Israel, which Moses received from the Lord at Mount Sinai. While he was inside the newly completed Tabernacle, Moses received the detailed laws of Leviticus that related to the sacrifices, the priesthood, the feast days, and other matters. Leviticus teaches that the way to God is through sacrifice and that one must be holy to walk with God. The book of Leviticus had special relevance to the priests, giving them a manual by which to guide Israel.

INTRODUCTION TO LEVITICUS

Authorship and Date of Leviticus

Moses wrote the book of Leviticus about one year after the exodus from Egypt. Therefore, a date of 1444 B.C. would be fairly accurate.

Purpose of Leviticus

The purpose of Leviticus is twofold: (1) to teach the nation of Israel the way to God, and (2) to teach them how to walk with God. This book was given to direct Israel to live as a holy nation in fellowship with a holy God. It was part of a code of law for the total well-being of the nation. For believers today the book gives insight into approaching God in worship and the need for holy living.

Special Considerations on Leviticus

The discussion under this same heading for Exodus applies to Leviticus as well.

SUMMARY OF LEVITICUS

The Way to God Is Through Sacrifice (Chaps. 1–10)

Leviticus

Basic Outline of Leviticus

I. The Way to God Is Through Sacrifice (chaps. 1–10)

    A. The Offerings and Their Regulations (1–7)

    B. The Consecration and Duties of the Priests (8–10)

II. Israel's Walk with God in Fellowship (chaps. 11–27)

    A. The Daily Lives of God's People (11–22)

    B. The Festivals of God's People (23–25)

    C. Promises and Warnings to God's People (26–27)

Important Data About Leviticus

1. Key Words: Holy and holiness; clean and unclean; atonement
2. Key Chapter: 11—The requirement to be holy
3. Key Verses: 11:44—The command to be holy because the Lord is holy; 17:11—The need to shed blood to cover sin
4. Key Characters: Moses, Aaron, and the sons of Aaron
5. Meaning of "Leviticus": Describes the book as directions for the rituals associated with the Levitical priesthood
6. Geography of Leviticus: The region of Mount Sinai

The Offerings and Their Regulations (1–7)

Once the Tabernacle was completed, offerings became part of the daily life of Israel. Since God was holy and Israel was sinful, it was necessary to make atonement ("a covering") for sin through the sacrifice of animals. This section records the different kinds of offerings that were part of Israel's worship experience.

The Burnt Offering (1:1–17)

This offering was the most common of the sacrifices and was to atone for the sin of the individual. The law demanded that the worshiper bring an unblemished male to be sacrificed, since that was considered the most valuable kind of offering. There was some flexibility on which kind of animal could be brought, depending on the financial condition of the person involved. He was to bring a bullock unless he was poor, and then a dove or pigeon would suffice (1:5, 14). When the offering was brought to the door of the Tabernacle, the priests followed the divinely revealed procedure.

> The offerer was to bring the animal to the priest in the courtyard surrounding the Tabernacle. Before killing the animal the offerer was to place his hand on its head, identifying it as his substitute. After it was killed, the priest was to sprinkle its blood on all sides of the altar. The offerer then had to skin the animal and chop it in pieces in preparation for the sacrifice. The entire animal except the skin, which was given to the priest, was burned on the altar.[10]

The Meal Offering (2:1–16)

This offering was flour or grain. Though detail is lacking, it was evidently to express thankfulness and dedication to God.

The Peace Offering (3:1–17)

This voluntary offering provided the Israelites an opportunity to express their desire to fellowship with the Lord. An unblemished male or female from the flocks or herds could be used. The offerer received part of the sacrificed animal to enjoy as a festive meal.

The Sin Offering (4:1–5:13)

The main purpose of this offering was to deal with a situation where purification was needed. It was employed at the dedication of the Tabernacle to purify the altar (9:8–11); it was part of the annual Day of Atonement

▲ Bedouin encampment in the Sinai desert, near the Red Sea.

16:11–14); and it was used for other purification needs (5:1–13).

The Trespass Offering (5:14–6:7)

If an individual violated the law by taking something that belonged to the Lord (such as the tithe) or man (such as property), he was required to bring a ram without blemish as a sacrifice. This offering was to be accompanied by proper restitution.

The Laws Regulating the Offerings (6:8–7:38)

The offerings are given again with regulations on the way they were to be presented.

The Consecration and Duties of the Priests (8–10)

When the Tabernacle was finally completed, Aaron and his sons were anointed (set apart) as priests by Moses (8:1–36). This act of consecration took one week and was followed immediately by a special time for setting apart Aaron as the high priest of Israel (9:1–24). But in these days of dedication two of Aaron's sons, Nadab and Abihu, were struck dead by the Lord at the Tabernacle. They had offered "strange fire before the Lord" (10:1). This may refer to fire unauthorized by Aaron or Moses, or perhaps it may have some connection to heathen practices they were using. Whatever it was, they had violated God's instructions. It has been suggested also that they may have been drunk, since Aaron was warned immediately about drinking wine or strong drink (10:9).

Israel's Walk with God in Fellowship (chaps. 11–27)

The Daily Lives of God's People (11–22)

In this section instruction is given on how Israel could be holy in their daily practices and so live in fellowship with the Lord, who is holy (11:44; 19:2). Great emphasis is placed on what was "clean" and what was "unclean." Something "clean" was thought to be pure. God wanted His people to be separated from physical and spiritual pollution.

The law spoke to every area of life. God was interested in the total well-being of His nation. What Israel ate mattered to Him (compare 11:1–47 with Deut. 14:3–21). Distinction was made between clean animals that could be eaten and unclean animals that were not to be part of their diet. (Some animals were identified as unclean because they were disease carriers, whereas others may have been so designated because of their associations with pagan worship.)

Regulations were given to govern activity at the birth of a child, and so the rites of purification and circumcision were given (12:1–8). God gave detailed instructions for identifying and dealing with a variety of skin diseases, a sort of medical handbook for the priests (13:1–15:33). God was equally precise on what constituted sinful sexual practices (18:1–30) and what God expected from them in their relationships with their neighbors (19:1–37).

Specific guidelines were given for the Day of Atonement, that day when national sin was atoned for (16:1–34). On this day only Israel's high priest would enter the holy of holies with the blood of a sacrificed bullock. He would sprinkle the blood on the mercy seat (the lid of the Ark of the Covenant; Ex. 25:17–22) first for himself and then return later with blood for the people's sin.

The Festivals of God's People (23–25)

The Sabbath was the key assembly of Israel. Every seventh day was a sacred day of rest and worship (23:1–4). The Sabbath was a sign of the Mosaic Covenant and a constant reminder to Israel of their special relationship with God (Ex. 31:13–17). However, seven feasts were to be part of Israel's annual life.

The Spring Festivals (23:5–22)

The *Passover* was the most important of all the festivals, marking the start of the year and reminding Israel of God's deliverance from Egypt. *Unleavened Bread* reminded them of their deliverance from slavery and *Firstfruit* celebrated God's goodness. *Pentecost* (Weeks) celebrated the harvest.

The Fall Festivals (23:23–44)

The *Feast of Trumpets* was a solemn assembly in which sacrifice and offering were the priorities. The *Day of Atonement* was the day the nation's sins were atoned for. *Tabernacle* was the joyous festival that recalled God's deliverance from Egypt and provision in the wilderness.

The Sabbath Year and Year of Jubilee
(24:1–25:55)
Every seventh year the land of Israel was to be given rest and to lie fallow. This was not only good agricultural procedure, but was also a test of Israel's faith and obedience. All Hebrew slaves were to be set free as well. Every fifty years was the Year of Jubilee. During this year, which began on the Day of Atonement, all land was to be at rest, and all land that had been sold was to be returned to its original owner (so keeping the land perpetually within the original tribe that owned it).

Promises and Warnings to God's People (26–27)

This section is particularly important because it details the steps of discipline God would take against Israel if they disobeyed Him. Chapter 26 provides the backdrop for many of God's future dealings with Israel and the messages of the prophets.

5. Numbers & Deuteronomy

NUMBERS

INTRODUCTION TO NUMBERS

Authorship and Date of Numbers

Moses wrote the book of Numbers as an eye-witness to the events recorded in it. Numbers concludes with Israel ready to enter and conquer Canaan. Since this conquest began just after Moses' death in 1405, a date of about 1406 B.C. is given.

Purpose of Numbers

Numbers was written to record Israel's history from their departure from Mount Sinai to their arrival in Moab on the east side of the Jordan River. Numbers continues the account of God's faithfulness in making of Abraham a "great nation." The land of Canaan would be Israel's in spite of this record of unbelief and unfaithfulness on Israel's part.

Special Considerations on Numbers

Years Covered by Numbers

The book of Numbers covers a period of forty years. However, very little information is actually recorded for most of that time. Much of the forty years was spent in aimless wandering.

Important Data About Numbers

1. Key Word: Wandering
2. Key Chapter: 14—Unbelief at Kadesh-barnea
3. Key Verses: 14:26–32
4. Key Characters: Moses, Aaron, Joshua, Caleb, Korah, and Balaam
5. Meaning of "Numbers": Title of this book reflects the two times when a census was taken of Israel
6. Geography of Numbers: Mount Sinai, the wilderness, Kadesh-barnea, the plains of Moab

Numbers

Background Points on Numbers

In order to move several million people (with their belongings and livestock) from Mount Sinai to Canaan, certain organizational steps had to be taken. Israel was arranged by tribes around the Tabernacle, which was at the center of the camp. There was a fixed marching and camping order. Each tribe knew when to leave as the nation broke camp and marched, and where to set up camp when the march ended. The tribe of Levi (with its subdivisions of Merari, Gershon, and Kohath) camped nearest the Tabernacle. The other tribes camped around the Tabernacle to the four points of the compass. On each side there was one "standard bearer" tribe along with two other tribes. As it turned out, the nation learned the marching and camping order very well, since they spent forty years doing it.

SUMMARY OF NUMBERS

The Journey from Sinai to Kadesh-Barnea (chaps. 1–12)

The Preparation for the Journey (1–9)
The First Numbering of the People (1:1–4:49)

After spending about a year at Mount Sinai, the nation of Israel was ready to conquer Canaan. Since Israel was going to have to fight against the nations in Canaan it was necessary to discover how many Israelites were able to go to war (1:3). The total number of men who were at least twenty years old and capable of fighting was 603,550 (1:46). All the tribes except Levi were counted. The Levites were not numbered because they were not to go to war (1:47).

The tribe of Levi was selected by God to be those special people to care for the Tabernacle and assist in the worship of the Lord (1:50–53). At the time of the tenth plague on Egypt when God preserved the firstborn of Israel, the Lord declared that the firstborn belonged to Him (Ex. 13:2). Now, the Levites were to belong to God in a special way (Num. 3:11–13, 45). All the firstborn had to be redeemed with a special price paid to the priests and Levites (18:16–17).

The Instructing of the People (5:1–9:23)
Once again the Israelites were reminded that they were to be clean because God dwelt among them. Emphasis was made on the need to be separate from that which was unclean and to be holy unto the Lord.

The Journey to Kadesh-Barnea (10–12)
The First Stage of the Journey (10:1–36)
The Israelites finally left Mount Sinai (10:11). On the journey, the people would be guided not only by the pillar of cloud (9:15–23), but also by the sounding of silver trumpets (10:2–9). In this way more than 2 million people would know when to leave, when to set up camp, when to go to war, and when to assemble together.

Rebellion Against Moses (11:1–12:16)
Although the Lord had graciously cared for Israel for more than a year, they repeatedly

The Mountains of Moab from the Dead Sea.

murmured and complained against His provisions for them. Complaining is an attack on the love and character of God and is viewed very seriously by God (cf. 1 Cor. 10:5–11). And Israel paid a high price for her ungrateful spirit. The trouble recorded here probably began with complaints from the non-Israelites on the outskirts of the camp (11:4). The complaint was against God's miraculous provision of food, the manna (11:6). This rebellious attitude was immediately judged. Later, the attitude of insubordination moved closer to home as Moses' own sister, Miriam, and his brother, Aaron, challenged Moses' authority (12:1). God moved immediately into the situ-

Plan of the Camp of Israel and order of Departure

NORTH—FOURTH DIVISION—CAMP OF DAN
157,600

DAN
62,700

ASHER
41,500

AND

NAPHTHALI
53,400

WEST—THIRD DIVISION—CAMP OF EPHRAIM
108,100

EAST—FIRST DIVISION—CAMP OF JUDAH
186,400

BENJAMIN
35,400

EPHRAIM
40,500

AND

MANASSEH
32,200

MERARITES
3,200

GERSHONITES
2,650

COURT OF
THE TABERNACLE

MOSES, AARON
AND THE PRIESTS

KOHATHITES
2,750

ISSACHAR
54,400

JUDAH
74,600

AND

ZEBULUN
57,400

GAD
45,650

AND

SIMEON
59,300

REUBEN
46,500

SOUTH—SECOND DIVISION—CAMP OF REUBEN
151,450

14 cubits   14 cubits   5 cubits

5 cubits

5 cubits

5 cubits   10 cubits   5 cubits
20 cubits

Order of Departure

1. The Ark, Moses, Aaron
2. Judah and tribes
3. Gershon and Merari
4. Reuben and tribes
5. Kohath
6. Ephraim and tribes
7. Dan and tribes
8. The "Mixed Multitude"

ation, making clear that Moses was indeed special and that he was Israel's leader (12:6–8). But these incidents of rebellion revealed an attitude that caused Israel's great failure at Kadesh-barnea.

Israel in the Wilderness— the Time of Transition (chaps. 13–19)

The Crisis of Unbelief at Kadesh-barnea (13–14)

When Israel arrived at Kadesh-barnea, twelve spies were sent into the land of Canaan to observe the conditions of the land and the people. Deuteronomy 1:22 makes clear that the people, not God, originated the idea of sending these spies into the land. After spending forty days in Canaan (13:25), they all returned with glowing reports on the fertility of the land (13:27). They agreed that the peoples of Canaan were mighty, living in fortified cities. But ten of the spies discouraged the people of Israel by declaring that it was impossible to possess the land. Only two spies, Joshua and Caleb, encouraged the people by reminding them that God would give them the land (13:30; 14:8). But the people, who had repeatedly doubted God's love and had complained against Him, responded in fear and unbelief. They spoke against the Lord Himself (14:3) as well as against Moses (14:2). They intended to kill Moses and return to Egypt (14:4, 10). The rebellion did not succeed, but because of their blatant unbelief, God declared that the rebels would not enter the Promised Land. Israel as a result would spend forty years aimlessly wandering in the wilderness until that generation died (14:23, 27–35). That generation lost the

Priestly line in Israel

Levi

Gershon   Kohath   Merari

Aaron

Eleazar   Ithamar   Nadab   Abihu

Levites were descendants of Jacob's third son, Levi (Gen. 46). Levi had three sons: Gershon, Kohath, and Merari (Num. 3:17). Sometimes men were identified by these sons (e.g. Gershonites). Aaron was a descendant of Levi's son Kohath. The priestly line came only from Aaron. Therefore, all priests were Levites, but very few Levites were priests. In the days of King David, the priesthood was divided into twenty-four groups— sixteen from the line of Eleazar and eight from the line of Ithamar (1 Chron. 24).

blessing of God, but they did not destroy His purpose of making Israel a "great nation" (Gen. 12:3).

Laws After the Crisis (15)

Once again Israel was reminded to be holy (15:40). And again Israel was given information about making offerings for sin.

Israel's Complaints in the Wilderness

Scripture	Israel's Complaint	Moses' Response	God's Response
Ex. 14:11	Grumbled at the sight of Pharaoh's army	Encouraged Israel to trust God	Delivered Israel
Ex. 15:24	Grumbled about the bitter water	Cried out to God	"Healed" the water
Ex. 16:2	Grumbled about the lack of food	Rebuked Israel	Supplied manna
Ex. 17:2	Grumbled about the lack of water	Prayed to the Lord	Water from the rock
Num. 11:1	Grumbled about God's provision of food	Anger and prayer	Judgment
Num. 14:2	Grumbled about Moses' leadership. Can't possess Canaan	Pled with Israel, prayed to the Lord	Judgment
Num. 16:2	Grumbled about Moses' leadership	Rebuked and prayed	Judgment
Num. 16:41	Grumbled about Moses	Prayed	Judgment
Num. 20:2	Grumbled about Moses and a lack of water	Rebuked Israel Struck rock	Supplied water
Num. 21:4	Grumbled about Moses and the manna	No response	Judgment

The Great Rebellion of Korah (16)

This challenging of Moses' leadership was particularly critical because it was a rebellion by leaders. Motivated by jealousy, Korah (a Levite) and 250 important leaders in Israel openly challenged Moses' authority. In response, Moses correctly noted that this rebellion was really a challenge against God, since God Himself had clearly placed Moses in this postion (16:11). God immediately judged the rebels by having the earth open up and killing them (16:31–35).

Though the hand of God was obvious in the matter, the attitude of many in Israel was still evil and rebellious (16:41).

The Aftermath of the Rebellion (17–19)

Because of the challenging of His leaders, God confirmed that the priesthood did in fact belong to Aaron and his family (17:1–13). Additional information is given regarding the provisions for the priests (18:1–32).

The Journey from Kadesh-barnea to Moab (chaps. 20–36)

Incidents on the Way to Moab (20–21)

After the years of discipline were over, God brought Israel back to the place of their failure (Kadesh-barnea) to begin again. Both Miriam and Aaron died at this time (20:1, 28). Aaron's son Eleazar became the new high priest of Israel.

Failure was still to be associated with Kadesh-barnea. To provide water for Israel, God commanded Moses to speak to a rock and water would come out. But in the presence of the people, Moses disobeyed God, striking the rock in his anger instead of speaking to it (20:10–11). Because of this disobedience, God would not allow Moses to enter Canaan (20:12).

When Israel finally arrived on the east side of the Jordan River, they were met by hostile peoples. In the days that followed, Israel defeated Sihon, king of the Amorites (21:21–25), and Og, king of Bashan (21:33–35). Much of the east side of the Jordan, therefore, fell under Israelite control.

The Incident with the Prophet Balaam (22–25)

When Balak, the king of Moab, saw Israel easily defeat the other kings of the area, he realized that he had no hope of a military victory over Israel. He therefore hired a pagan prophet by the name of Balaam, promising great reward if he would pronounce a curse on Israel. But when God appeared to Balaam and warned him not to do so, Balaam was afraid and refused to curse Israel. But Balaam wanted the

Relief of the Canaanite deity Baal.

wealth offered by King Balak, and, instead of cursing Israel, he counseled Balak to get Israel involved in the degraded fertility religion of Baal. Such involvement would bring the wrath of the Lord on Israel, and Balak could watch Israel's God destroy His own people. The plan partially worked (25:1–9; 31:16). For his evil counsel, Balaam was later executed by Israel (31:8). Balaam is used by Bible writers as a negative example of one who was both covetous and a compromiser (cf. 2 Pet. 2:15; Jude 11; Rev. 2:14).

The New Numbering of the People of Israel (26–27)

As Israel readied to enter Canaan and fight, it was necessary again to take a census to determine the size of the army. The total in this census was 601,730, several thousand less than the first census. Normally a significant increase would have been expected, but the judgments of the forty years in the wilderness had had their effect.

The New Instructing of Israel (28–36)

Three noteworthy events took place at this point. First, Joshua was selected by God to be Israel's next leader (27:18–23). Joshua was publicly commissioned so there would be no power struggle at the death of Moses. Second, the tribes of Reuben, Gad, and half of the tribe of Manasseh requested and were granted permission to settle on the east side of the Jordan River (32:1–33). This territory was not part of the land area given Israel under the Abrahamic Covenant. Third, Moses set aside six "cities of refuge" (35:1–34). These cities were places where those who were guilty of accidentally killing another person could be protected.

With the ending of the book of Numbers, Israel is poised and ready to possess the land of promise. The next foundational book, Joshua, records the taking of the land. (For further discussion on the foreign nations with whom Israel had dealings, see "Israel and the Nations," page 98.)

DEUTERONOMY

The book of Deuteronomy complements Numbers; it does not advance the story of the Old Testament. The messages of this book were given by Moses as Israel camped in the plains of Moab. Moses was about to die, and a new generation in Israel (which was not born until after Israel left Mount Sinai) needed some special instruction in the law of God. So these words of Moses were a needed reminder to all Israel, although they were particularly important to the new generation.

INTRODUCTION TO DEUTERONOMY

Authorship and Date of Deuteronomy

Most likely Moses wrote the book of Deuteronomy about the same time as Numbers. Therefore, a date of 1405 B.C. is given for Deuteronomy.

Purpose of Deuteronomy

The main purpose of the book is to remind Israel of their special relationship to God. They were the covenant people and were to obey His laws. Israel was reminded in Deuteronomy of the privileged position that they had and the resulting responsibility to serve God faithfully and to be holy. In these messages Moses pled with the people to obey the commandments. His pleas to the nation were based on several facts: (1) God's good-

Important Data About Dueteronomy

1. Key Words: Observe, do, keep, and obey
2. Key Chapter: 8—Exhortation to obey and keep the covenant with God
3. Key Verses: 10:12–13— A reminder to fear, love, and obey the Lord God
4. Key Characters: Moses and Joshua
5. Meaning of "Deuteronomy": "*deuter*" = second ; "*nomos*" = law; a second giving of the law
6. Geography of Deuteronomy: The plains of Moab, east of the Jordan River

ness to them in the past (4:32–40); (2) God's goodness to them in the recent wilderness experience (29:5–9); (3) Israel's responsibility to be a good testimony to the nations of the earth (4:6–7); (4) God's love which had been poured out on them (7:7–11); (5) God's sure promise of blessing (7:12–14); and (6) God's warnings of certain judgment for disobedience (29:24–28).

Special Considerations on Deuteronomy

The discussion under this same heading for Numbers applies to Deuteronomy as well.

SUMMARY OF DEUTERONOMY

Moses Reviews Israel's Journey from Sinai to the Plains of Moab (chaps. 1–4)

To the new generation Moses gave the authoritative account of Israel's recent history. Beginning at Mount Sinai and concluding with the arrival in the plains of Moab, Moses spoke of God's great power and faithfulness as well as Israel's unbelief and failure. He reminded Israel of God's provision and protection. He also reminded them that the way to blessing is through obedience.

Deuteronomy

Basic Outline of Deuteronomy

I. Moses Reviews Israel's Journey from Sinai to the Plains of Moab (chaps. 1–4)

II. Moses Reviews and Expands the Law for the New Generation (chaps. 4–26)

III. Moses Reviews Israel's Covenant Relationship with God (chaps. 27–30)

IV. The Final Ministry of Moses (chaps. 31–34)

The Plains of Moab

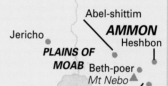

MEDITERRANEAN SEA

Mt Ebal

● Shechem

Mt Gerizim

River Jordan

GILEAD

Abel-shittim

AMMON

Heshbon

Jericho ●

PLAINS OF MOAB

Beth-poer ●

Mt Nebo

Pisgah

DEAD SEA

NEGEB

MOAB

● Zoar

```
0    10    20   km
├────┼────┤
0    10   15 mi
```

Kadesh-banea
●

Moses Reviews and Expands the Law for the New Generation (chaps. 4–26)

The majority of the book falls in this section. It deals with some highly significant matters that will greatly affect the well-being of the nation in the days ahead.

Absolutely essential to Israel's well-being was their knowledge of God's law (their constitution). The priests and Levites functioned as teachers of this law. But even more significant than the instructions by these men were the teachings of the parents. Parents were to be the key in the communication of God's truth from generation to generation (6:1–9). Parents were to teach their children to fear the Lord and to love the Lord (6:2, 5, 12). They were to be diligent in this task. Later on, parents in Israel would violate this instruction with the result that whole generations would grow up not "knowing the Lord" (Judg. 2:10).

Another vital issue given by Moses in this message concerned Israel's relationship to the Canaanites (7:1–6). Two critical orders were given. First, Israel was to destroy utterly and completely every Canaanite in the land, making no treaty of any kind with them. (For a further discussion of this radical invasion policy, see "The Extermination of the Canaanites," page 89.) Second, there was to be no intermarriage with the Canaanites. During the several years that it would take to conquer Canaan, intermarriage would have been a possibility. But intermarriage would bring idolatry with it. As it turned out, both of these orders were violated numerous times by Israel, and the results were tragic (Judg. 1:28; 2:11–12).

In this message, Moses also revealed a unique fact about the Promised Land (11:10–17), which would be referred to again and again by the prophets of Israel. This land could not be irrigated like the land of Egypt. With the Jordan River hundreds of feet below sea level, it was not a source of water for crops or grazing areas. This land would be totally dependent on the rains. God promised that if Israel obeyed Him, He would always bring rain for her crops and cattle. He would withhold rain only if Israel was disobedient to His law. Therefore, drought (with the eventual famine) was a spiritual issue in Israel and was designed to be a clear, visible indicator that God was displeased because of her disobedience (e.g., see Joel 2:10–12; Hag. 2:11; Jer. 14:1).

Other subjects discussed by Moses in this message included the absolute necessity of removing all idolatry from Canaan (chap. 12), the great faithfulness of God (8–9), the matter of divorce (24), the positions of the prophet (13–18) and the kings (17), and additional information on Israel's relationships with foreign nations (20).

Moses Reviews Israel's Covenant Relationship with God (chaps. 27–30)

Since the covenant made at Mount Sinai was a "conditional covenant," there were blessings and curses attached to it. Curses were given for breaking the law and blessings were given for being obedient to it (chaps. 27–28). Extremely significant in this section is the discussion of the Palestinian Covenant, which is a subdivision of the unconditional Abrahamic Covenant. The Palestinian

The Dead Sea, with the Mountains of Moab beyond. Moses got no closer than Moab to Canaan.

Covenant gave the "title deed" of Canaan to the nation of Israel. It was and always would be Israel's land. The borders of the land were defined in the law. However, Israel's sin and disobedience would affect this covenant. Although disobedience would not annul the covenant, Israel could lose their right to live on the land. But it was also clear that in the future, Israel would be converted and restored to the land (see Gen. 17:7–8; 13:14–17; Deut. 28:63–68; 30:1–10; Lev. 26:32–33; Ezek. 36:24–29; 37:11–14; 34:11–31; Rom. 11:26–27).

The Final Ministry of Moses (chaps. 31–34)

After Moses communicated the needed information to the new generation, he knew it was his time to die (31:2). Joshua would now take over and lead the people (31:14, 23). Moses finished his literary task (31:24–26), blessed the people (33:1), and climbed Mount Nebo to see the land of promise (34:1–4). Moses then died, and the nation of Israel entered a new phase in its national life. Joshua and the people readied themselves for entering and conquering Canaan.

Boundaries of the
Promised Land

Mt Hor

Byblos
Aphekah
Lebo-hamath

Sidon
Damascus

Dan

Achzib
Kadesh
Hazor
Acco   Ramah   Chinnereth
Rehob   *Sea of*   Ashtaroth
Nahalol   Aphek   *Chinnereth*
Kitron

Megiddo   Ain
Dor   Jezreel
Taanach   Beth-shan   Ramoth-gilead
Ibleam   Jabesh-gilead

Mount Ebal
Shechem   Succoth
Mount Gerizim

G R E A T   S E A

Aphek   Shiloh   A M M O N
Gezer   Bethel Gilgal
Aijalon   Gibeon
Ashdod   Ekron   Jebus   Heshbon
Beth-   (Jerusalem)
Ashkelon   Gath- shemesh   Bethlehem   Medeba
Gaza   Dibon
Lachish   Hebron   Aroer
Debir

NUMBERS 34:1–2
(Joshua 15:1–2)
(Ezekiel 47:15–20)

Beersheba

Jordan

Salt Sea

M O A B

Brook of Egypt   *Mount Halak*   Zoar

Tamar

Kadesh-barnea   E D O M

| 0 | 25 | 50 km |
| 0 | 10 | 20 | 30 miles |

Area controlled
by Israelites

PHILISTIA

6.

Joshua

INTRODUCTION TO JOSHUA

Authorship and Date of Joshua

Among conservative scholars opinion is divided on the authorship of this book. Jewish tradition assigns the book to Joshua. It is clear that Joshua did write some things found in this book (cf. 18:9; 24:26). The author was surely an eyewitness of these events, as the details given reflect a precise knowledge of events (for example, 3:14–17; 4:19–20; 5:1–12; 6:12–15). Furthermore, the author was living at the time of these events because of certain statements made, such as that Rahab was still living (6:25). It is clear that a few verses would not have been written by Joshua (24:29–30; 24:31–33). But these

Archaeologists' discoveries at Jericho, one of the world's most ancient cities.

Joshua

I. Possessing the Land (chaps. 1–12)

  A. The Entrance into Canaan (1–5)

  B. The Conquering of Canaan (6–12)

II. Dividing the Land (chaps. 13–24)

  A. The Inheritances of the Tribes (13–22)

  B. The Last Messages of Joshua (23–24)

Important Data About Joshua

1. Key Word: Victory
2. Key Chapter: 6—The beginning of the conquest
3. Key Verses: 1:5–8; 21:43–45; 24:15
4. Key Characters: Joshua and Caleb
5. Meaning of "Joshua": Title reflects the key figure of the book
6. Geography of Joshua: The plains of Moab, Gilgal, and Canaan

verses could have been added to Joshua's writings by another without greatly affecting the authorship of Joshua. Although there is some debate on this matter, this study assigns the authorship to Joshua with a date of about 1390 B.C.

Purpose of Joshua

The purpose of Joshua is to record the conquest of the land of Canaan by Israel and therefore show the faithfulness of God in making of Abraham "a great nation."

Special Considerations on Joshua

Years Covered by Joshua

The book of Joshua covers about thirty years o Israel's history. However, the emphasis is o the five to seven years (based on the testimony of Caleb, 14:6–11) of Joshua's military activi ties. After the conclusion of the conquest c Canaan by Joshua, the eighty-five-year-ol Caleb recalled that he was forty years old whe he went and spied out the land in the days o Moses (Num. 13:6). Out of the forty-five year that followed that event (between the ages o forty and eighty-five), thirty-eight or thirty nine of those years were spent wandering i the wilderness, leaving five to seven years fo the conquest under Joshua.

Background Points on Joshua

(a) Joshua's Assigned Tasks

The first task given to Joshua was to destro Canaanite power in the land. Strong, fortifie cities and the key Canaanite kings were th targets of Joshua. Joshua would not hav had time to search out every single Canaan ite in the land and destroy him. But he faith fully destroyed the key cities. On both the eas

The Cave of Machpelah, Hebron, by tradition the burial place of the patriarchs of Israel.

and the west side of the Jordan River Joshua destroyed a total of thirty-one kings (12:24). Joshua's second responsibility was to divide up the land among the tribes of Israel. Once the land was parceled out among the tribes, it became the responsibility of each individual tribe to enter its territory and eliminate all the Canaanites left there. Joshua obeyed the Lord and completed his assigned tasks. Unfortunately, as history reveals, Israel did not.

(b) Israel's Foreign Policy
In Deuteronomy 7 and 20, Israel's relationships with other nations are detailed. Israel could enter into restricted treaties with nations who lived outside the boundaries of the land given in the covenant. But nations inside of those boundaries were to be totally destroyed, and no treaties or covenants could be made with them. (See "The Extermination of the Canaanites," page 89)

SUMMARY OF JOSHUA

Possessing the Land (chaps. 1–12)

The Entrance into Canaan (1–5)
God is never thwarted by the death of His servants. Although the death of Moses must have been a depressing event to Joshua and Israel, God immediately appeared to Joshua, bringing encouragement to him (1:5). Joshua was guaranteed of God's presence and blessing (1:1–9).

In preparation for entering Canaan, two

men were sent into the area near Jericho to spy it out. When the mission of the spies was discovered by the Canaanites, they were protected by a prostitute named Rahab. Rahab not only protected them but also greatly encouraged them by revealing that the mighty peoples of Canaan were absolutely terrified by Israel's presence on the east side of Jordan (2:8–11). This fulfilled God's promise to bring great fear on the people of the land (cf. Deut. 2:25; 11:25). When Jericho was destroyed, the believing Rahab was spared (6:17, 25). She would later marry a prince of the tribe of Judah and become an ancestor of Jesus Christ (Num. 7:12; 1 Chron. 2:10–15; Matt. 1:4–6). Rahab is an Old Testament illustration of the marvelous grace of God.

As Israel prepared to cross the Jordan River, God gave specific instructions that the Ark of the Covenant was to lead the people (a visible reminder that God keeps His covenants). The crossing of the Jordan River was an event to parallel the Red Sea crossing (3:5, 7). When the sandals of the priests carrying the Ark touched the water, the waters were immediately stopped and Israel crossed over on dry ground (3:14–17). After crossing the Jordan, Israel camped at Gilgal. Gilgal would be the base camp for Joshua, the people, and the army for several years.

Fear gripped the Canaanites in an even greater way after this supernaturally aided crossing (5:1). On the west side of the Jordan, several events took place before the conquest actually began. First, it was necessary to circumcise the males of Israel (5:2–9). Circumcision was the external sign of the Abrahamic Covenant, which the man of Israel bore on his body (Gen. 17:9–14; Acts 7:8). Also, Israel celebrated her first Passover in the new land and witnessed the end of the provision of manna (5:10–12). And finally, in preparation for the conquest, Joshua met the real commander of Israel's army, the Lord Himself (5:13–15).

The Conquering of Canaan (6–12)

These chapters give a greatly condensed account of the conquering of Canaan. During the next five to seven years Joshua would attack and defeat Canaanite strongholds, go back to rest at Gilgal, and then return to battle again. The conquest of Canaan took place in three stages. First, the conquest of central Canaan took place, which included such cities as Jericho and Ai. Second came the southern campaign, which brought about the defeat of such cities as Jerusalem and Hebron. Finally, the northern campaign centered on the Canaanite fortress city of Hazor.

The Victory in Central Canaan (6:1–8:35)

Though they were assured of victory in their battles, Israel had to obey God. The battle of Jericho was not won in the conventional way. It was won by doing it God's way. Jericho was a kind of "firstfruits" of the whole land and thus belonged to God (6:18–19). Normally the spoils of war went to the people, but not in this case. Because one man, Achan, appropriated for himself that which belonged to God, Israel suffered her only military defeat in the days of Joshua (7:4–5, 11–13, 20–21). After dealing with the issue of sin in the camp of Israel, Joshua and the people defeated Ai.

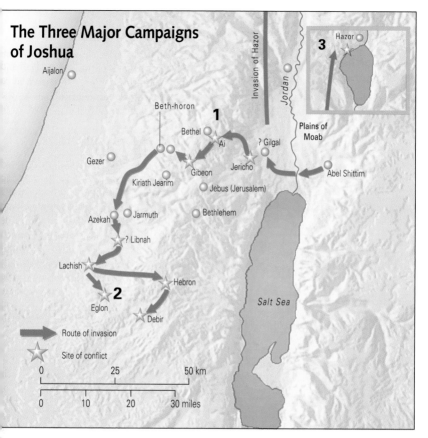

The Three Major Campaigns of Joshua

Aijalon

Beth-horon

1

Bethel

Ai

Gezer

Gibeon

Jericho

? Gilgal

Kiriath Jearim

Jebus (Jerusalem)

Azekah

Jarmuth

Bethlehem

? Libnah

Lachish

Hebron

2

Eglon

Debir

Invasion of Hazor

Jordan

Plains of Moab

3

Hazor

Abel Shittim

Salt Sea

Route of invasion

Site of conflict

0 — 25 — 50 km

0 — 10 — 20 — 30 miles

The Victory over the Southern Kings (9:1–10:43)

Unfortunately the incident at Ai was not the only failure of Israel. They failed to "ask for the counsel of the Lord" (9:14) and ended up in covenant with the Gibeonites, a people who lived inside the borders of the land. But God used even that failure to open up the southern part of the land. City after city fell before Joshua and the Israelites (10:1–43).

The Victory over the Northern Kings (11:1–12:24)

In order to repel Israel, the remnants of the south along with mighty kings of the north formed an alliance to face Joshua. Joshua had never faced such a formidable army (11:4–5). But God encouraged Joshua, and a great victory was given to Israel (11:6–8).

The Northern Campaigns

Sidon
Tyre
Kedesh
Hazor
Merom
Acco
Sea of Galilee
Shimron
JEZREEL VALLEY
Battle
Canaanite army
Israelite army Beth-shan
From Gilgal

The book then gives a summary of the conquests on both sides of the Jordan (12:1–24), noting that much territory still needed to be conquered (by the individual tribes, after the dividing up of the land, 13:1).

Dividing the Land (chaps. 13–24)

The Inheritances of the Tribes (13–22)

Dividing up the land would be done by the casting of lots (Num. 26:52–55; 33:54–55). And the size of the tribe would also be a consideration. Historically the dividing of the land occurred in three steps. First was the distribution of the land on the east side of the Jordan under the direction of Moses (Reuben, Gad, and half of Manasseh). The second step in the distribution of the land took place at Gilgal

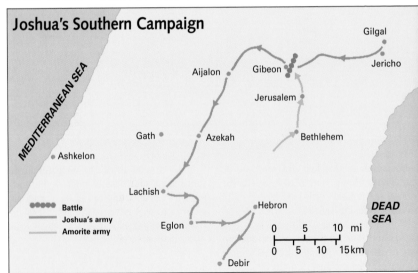

Joshua's Southern Campaign

Gilgal
Jericho
Aijalon   Gibeon
Jerusalem
MEDITERRANEAN SEA
Gath   Azekah   Bethlehem
Ashkelon
Lachish
Hebron   **DEAD SEA**
Eglon
0   5   10 mi
0   5   10   15 km
Debir

Battle
Joshua's army
Amorite army

Land allocated to the Tribes of Israel

GREAT SEA

Tyre

DAN
Dan (Laish)

Kedesh

ASHER

NAPHTALI

ZEBULUN

Sea of Chinnereth

Golan

Shimron
Endor

MANASSEH

Megiddo
ISSACHAR

Ramoth-gilead

MANASSEH

Jordan

Shechem

Succoth

Beth-dagon

EPHRAIM
Shiloh

DAN
Bethel

GAD

BENJAMIN
Gibeah
Jericho

Jebus (Jerusalem)
Heshbon
Bezer

JUDAH
REUBEN

Gaza
Hebron

Salt Sea

Beersheba

MOAB

SIMEON

Brook of Egypt

0   25   50 km

0   10   20   30 miles

----- Probable boundary of tribe of Israel
→ Migration of the tribe of Dan
◎ City of refuge

E   D   O   M

Probable site of Shiloh, where Joshua set up the Tabernacle after he had occupied the land.

with Joshua in charge (15:1–17:13). Judah, Ephraim, and the other half of Manasseh received their land at this time. The third step in land distribution took place at Shiloh, after Joshua set up the Tabernacle there. The seven remaining tribes received their territories at this time (18:11–19:48). It should be noted that the tribe of Joseph received a double portion of the land, as the possessor of the birth-right (1 Chron. 5:1–2). The double portion of the land is identified by Joseph's two sons, Ephraim and Manasseh.

The Last Messages of Joshua (23–24)

Before his death, Joshua exhorted the people to faithfully serve the Lord and to be obedient to His commands. As long as Joshua was alive, Israel remained faithful to the Lord.

The Extermination of the Canaanites

In Israel's first battle inside the boundaries of the Promised Land, they killed every human being except for Rahab and her family (Josh. 6:21). This total extermination of everyone in the city of Jericho was simply in obedience to a command of the Lord. The Lord had commanded that all Canaanites living within the designated land boundaries given to Israel were to be exterminated. ("Canaanite" is a general term used for the several different peoples who lived in that land.) No mercy was to be shown to them, and no treaties of any kind were to be made with them (Ex. 23:31–33; 34:11–17; Lev. 18:24–25; Deut. 7:1–2; 20:16–18). All of their religious images and artifacts were to be destroyed also. These people had been set apart for complete and utter destruction. Joshua and the Israelites were to carry out the Lord's command.

Some people have questioned the morality of God's command to exterminate the Canaanites. But the Scriptures and archaeology justify this command. The Canaanite society had become terribly degenerate. Their perverted religious practices had so polluted them that their iniquity was as great as it could be (cf. Gen. 15:16). They worshiped a large number of deities who were characterized by wicked behavior that in turn dictated the behavior of the Canaanites.

> The brutality, lust and abandon of Canaanite mythology is far worse than elsewhere in the Near East at the time. And the astounding characteristic of Canaanite deities, that they had no moral character whatever, must have brought out the worst traits in their devotees and entailed many of the most demoralizing practices of the time, such as sacred prostitution, child sacrifice and snake worship.[1]

Canaanite religion was basically a fertility religion. Since they were an agricultural society, the Canaanites were interested in fertility and production. Their gods (such as El and Baal) and their goddesses (such as Asherah, Anath, and Astarte) were fertility gods, whose activities affected the crops and the animals. It was believed that the perverted sexual relations among these gods and goddesses directly affected fertility on the earth. The gods themselves were supposedly stimulated to such relations by the perverted and depraved sexual activities of the Canaanites as they "worshiped" in the temples.[2]

Leviticus 18 is a key chapter in understanding the character of the Canaanites. This chapter details those sexual practices that were abhorrent to God, including adultery, incest, homosexuality, and bestiality. These practices characterized the people of Canaan (18:3, 24–28). Other evils, such as child sacrifice, were part of Canaanite life as well. The nations that inhabited the Promised Land were just as evil as the residents of Sodom and Gomorrah (Gen. 18; 19) or those people who lived in the days of Noah (Gen. 6:5; 11).

It was clear that Israel could have absolutely no contact with these people, or else Israel would become infected with the same moral and spiritual sickness. Israel was called repeatedly to be a holy people, different from the peoples who inhabited Canaan (Deut. 7:1–4). There was no room for compromise or coexistence. The Canaanites had evidently come to the place spiritually where they would never turn to the true God (like those mentioned in Rom. 1:24–28). A few, like Rahab of Jericho (Josh. 6:17), may have come to the God of Israel, but they were rare exceptions. And too, it should be noted that any Canaanite wishing to avoid death could have easily fled outside the borders of the Promised Land and been safe. The taking of the land under Joshua lasted about six years. A person could flee outside of the boundaries from anywhere in the land in two or three days.

It must also be remembered that God is sovereign. He is the great Creator and can do what He wishes with His creation. He has the right and the power to deal with those who violate His holy laws.

> God is a holy God. He demands that sin be punished. The Lord reserves the right to punish sin wherever it is found, whether it be in the immediate destruction of a city or the condemnation of the sinner at final judgment. It is only by the mercy and the grace of God that any sinner is permitted to live his life completely.[3]

7. Judges & Ruth

JUDGES

INTRODUCTION TO JUDGES

Authorship and Date of Judges

Unlike many of the books of the New Testament, which identify the author at the beginning of the letter, Old Testament authors are not so easily identified. Jewish and Christian tradition assign the book of Judges to Samuel, though there is some lack of certainty. Several times in the book the phrase "there was no king in Israel" is used. This suggests that the author was writing in a time when there *was* a king in Israel and was informing his readers of that important fact. The book also says that the Jebusites still were in control of Jerusalem (1:21), a situation that changed when David became king and removed them (2 Sam. 5:6). These statements, therefore, point to the real possibility that Judges was written during the monarchy, but before the days of David. The reign of Saul is the best estimate, and Samuel would fit very well. The authorship of Judges is assigned to Samuel, and the date of writing would then be about 1000 B.C.

Judges

Basic Outline of Judges

I. The Record of Incomplete Obedience (chaps. 1–3)

II. The Judges of Israel (chaps. 3–16)

III. Illustrations from the Era of the Judges (chaps. 17–21)

Timeline of Joshua and Judges

JOSHUA	"ELDERS"	JUDGES	
1405	1390	1375 …332 years…	1043
Entering	Death of	Israel's	Saul
of Canaan	Joshua (?)	First	Becomes
		Apostasy	King

Purpose of Judges

Judges was written to record the experiences of Israel during the era of the theocracy. The book sets forth great failures of Israel during this period.

Important Data About Judges

1. Key Word: Defeat
2. Key Chapter: 2—Gives the "cycle of the judges"
3. Key Verses: 2:11–19; 17:6; 21:25
4. Key Characters: Gideon, Samson, and Jephthah
5. Meaning of "Judges": Title reflects the key office in this period of Israel's history
6. Geography of Judges: Various locations within Israel

Special Considerations on Judges

Years Covered by Judges

The actual length of time for the period of the judges (the "era of the theocracy") is 332 years. The book of Judges is actually less than that since two of the men who served as judges are found in the book of 1 Samuel. One of the chronological problems in the Old Testament is associated with the book of Judges. When the total number of years given for the length of judgeships and of the years of oppression by foreign nations is added up, the figure is 407 years (75 more years than is available in Israel's history). The solution to this problem is accounted for by noting that there were overlaps in the judgeships; that is, more than one judge ruled at a time.[1]

Background Points on Judges

(a) The Concept of the Theocracy

Before Moses died, Joshua was selected by God to be Israel's leader. But no provision was made for a leader when Joshua died. Why? Because it was not God's intention to have His nation ruled by one man. Such leaders were necessary in the era when the nation was being formed (see chart "Eras of Old Testament History," page 21.) But once Israel had their "people," "law," and "land," God Himself was to be their supreme ruler (a "theocracy"). This was the ideal form of government for Israel and one that would bring the finest blessings and greatest satisfaction. (A monarchy or other form of government would be "second best.") In the theocracy, the people would live under God's law, with the priests being those who taught

Chronology of Israel's Judges

Judge	Scripture	Nation who oppressed them	Years	Years of Peace after Deliverance
Othniel	3:9–11	Mesopotamia	8	40
Ehud	3:12–30	Moabites	18	80
Shamgar	3:31	Philistines	?	?
Deborah (Barak)	4:4–5:3	Canaanites	20	40
Gideon	6:1–8:35	Midianites	7	40
Tola	10:1, 2	?	?	23
Jair	10:3–5	?	?	22
Jephthah	11:1–12:7	Ammonites	18	6
Ibzan	12:8–10	?	?	7
Elon	12:11, 12	?	?	10
Abdon	12:13–15	?	?	8
Samson	13:1–16:31	Philistines	40	20
Eli	1 Samuel	Philistines		
Samuel	1 Samuel	Philistines		

nd administered God's law. A theocracy is the ighest and best form of government, and one ay it will be reinstituted with the Lord Jesus Christ as supreme ruler.

b) The Position of the Judge

The judges appeared as significant people during the theocracy period. But they came on the scene only because of sin and failure. They were, in a sense, unnecessary to the theocracy. Judges were introduced when it became nec-essary to rescue Israel from bad situations—situations brought about because of Israel's sin. The judges' basic responsibilities were to deliver Israel from foreign oppressors and to curtail sin in Israel.

Judges were not like the kings who appeared later in Israel's history. They had less power than the kings (for example, judges could not tax people or keep a standing army). They governed much smaller geographic areas, often including the territories of just a few tribes.

Mount Tabor, site of Deborah's exploits.

And, unlike the kings, their position of rulership was not passed on to their descendants.

(c) Key Background Scriptures
Deuteronomy 7:1–4 commanded Israel to exterminate the Canaanites in the land and to refrain from any intermarriage with them. It was the violation of these commands that became the source of Israel's trouble in the theocracy. *Psalm 106:34–39* is a "divine commentary" on the era of the judges. It reveals the depths of Israel's sin, which included terrible immorality and human sacrifice. *Joshua 24:29–31* gives insight into how quickly Israel departed from the Lord after the death of Joshua. Israel served the Lord only in

Cycles of the Judges

SERVED
THE LORD

ISRAEL
DELIVERED

SINNED/
IDOLATRY

Judges 2:11–19

A JUDGE
RAISED UP

BECAME
SLAVES

CRIED TO
THE LORD

The Judges

Asher

Naphtali

Lake Huleh

Hazor

Sea of Chinnereth

Kishon

Zebulun

Kedesh

Mount Tabor

? Ophrah

GIDEON

Midian

JAIR

Megiddo

Hill of Moreh

Issachar

Taanach

Spring of Harod

Jezreel

Jordan

GILEAD

Tob

Abel-meholah

JEPHTHAH

Manasseh

Shechem

Mount Gerizim

Succoth

Jabbok

ABDON

Pirathon

Zererah

Penuel

? Shamir

TOLA

E p h r a i m

Shiloh

Jogbehah

Bethel

A M M O N

EBORAH

Aijalon

B e n j a m i n

? Gilgal

ELON

Ramah

? **EHUD**

ON

Timnah

Zorah

Kiriath-

Jebus

Jericho

Heshbon

AN

jearim

(Jerusalem)

Bethlehem

hkelon

PHILISTIA

J u d a h

M O A B

za

Hebron

S a l t   S e a

OTHNIEL

? Debir

Arnon

? **EHUD**   judge and home town

0   25   50 km

0   10   20   30 miles

those few years that followed Joshua's death when the "elders" who served with Joshua were still alive.

(d) The Cycle of the Judges
The era of the theocracy is clearly summarized in Judges 2:11–19. This "cycle" is repeated again and again during the 332 years of the theocracy.

SUMMARY OF JUDGES

The Record of Incomplete Obedience (chaps. 1–3)

In the days immediately after Joshua's military victories, Israel continued to obediently win battles over the Canaanites. But soon the Scripture text begins to record that the tribes "did not drive out the Canaanites who were living" in such and such an area (1:21, 27, 29–33). Instead, dominant Israel forced the Canaanites to serve them (1:28) in direct violation of God's command (Deut. 7:1). This disobedience was the seed that would bring forth a harvest of trouble for Israel.

The Judges of Israel (chaps. 3–16)

The book of Judges records seven apostasies of the nation of Israel during the theocracy. (An "apostasy" is a deliberate, knowledgeable turning away from the Lord.) In each of these cases Israel became enslaved to a foreign power, repented, and was delivered by a judge. Although much could be said about most of the judges, we will make only a brief summary statement. (For additional details about each judge, see the chart "Chronology of Israel's Judges," page 93.)

Othniel
He was the younger brother (or nephew) of the famous Caleb. Othniel was already known as a heroic individual, having taken part in the conquering of Canaan (Josh. 15:15–20). The presence of Othniel as the first judge makes clear that Israel did indeed depart quickly from the Lord after the death of Joshua.

Ehud
After enjoying forty years with no oppression, the Moabites subjugated some of Benjamin and Ephraim. Ehud, a leading man of Benjamin, assassinated the king of Moab and brought about deliverance for the oppressed area of Israel. After this deliverance, there were eighty years of rest for the people of Israel.

Shamgar
His efforts were directed toward the Philistines who lived southwest of Israel. Although not much is given about him, he must have been important in his day to be mentioned in the Scriptures.

Deborah (and Barak)
Deborah, a prophetess of God, was the judge, and Barak, an experienced general from the tribe of Naphtali, was the deliverer. Evidently God gave Barak victory over the iron chariots of the oppressing Canaanites by causing a heavy rain to make the battlefield muddy, thus bogging down the chariots (5:21).

Deborah and the Canaanites

Kedesh
Merom
Hazor
Chinnereth
Harosheth-Ha-Goiim
Sea of Chinnereth
Achshaph
Israelites gather
Mount Tabor
Jokneam
Dor
Megiddo
Canaanites gather

Israelites
Canaanites

0   10   20 km
0   4   8   12 miles
Location of Meroz is unknown

MACHIR
Jordan

thing to come from his house was his only child, a daughter. The normal reading of the text indicates that he did indeed sacrifice her—something God would never approve (note Ps. 106:37).

Ibzan, Elon, and Abdon
These three judges served in different areas of Israel. They were probably contemporaries of one another and perhaps served alongside Jephthah.

Samson
He was clearly not of the spiritual quality of a Daniel or a Joshua. But God gave Samson unusual strength in order to cause the oppressing Philistines great problems and make it impossible for them to overrun Israel.

Illustrations from the Era of the Judges (chaps. 17–21)

The events recorded in these chapters transpired at different times during the era of the theocracy. These accounts were selected to represent and illustrate the major sins of this era. They are not the only sins or necessarily the worst sins of this time. The religious apostasy (chaps. 17–18) occurred fairly early in the period of the judges. Baal worship was the primary sin of Israel, but not the only one. The worship of Baal precipitated many other sins. The moral degeneracy and the political anarchy (chaps. 19–21) show how far away from the "constitution" Israel did go. The immorality and disregard for human life illustrate the basic weakness of the theocracy—sinful man.

Gideon
After convincing Gideon through the use of three supernatural signs (6:21; 6:36; 7:15), God used him to deliver Israel from the Midianites. The battle itself evidenced God's working on Israel's behalf (7:19–22).

Tola and Jair
These two were probably contemporary judges; Tola served west of the Jordan, and Jair on the east side.

Jephthah
He liberated Israel from the Ammonites. But the fame of this judge comes from a vow he made to God before the battle. He promised to sacrifice to God the first thing that came out of his house upon returning from battle. The first

Israel and the Nations

The Amalekites

Amalek was a great-great-grandson of Abraham. He was the son of Eliphaz, who was the firstborn of Esau (Gen. 36:10, 12, 16; 1 Chron. 1:36). The descendants of Amalek settled in the desert area southwest of the Dead Sea and down into the Sinai Peninsula.

The first mention of the Amalekites was in connection with their attack on Moses and the Israelites at the time of the Exodus (Ex. 17:14; Deut. 25:17–19). Even though they were related to Israel (see chart "Nations Related to Israel," page 100), the Amalekites are always seen as bitter enemies of God's people (Num. 14:45; 1 Sam. 30:1–2). God executed judgment on these people especially at the hands of Saul and David (1 Sam. 15:1– 9; 30:16–20). They are last heard of in the days of King Hezekiah (1 Chron. 4:43). It should be noted that Moses does mention the Amalekites long before Amalek was born (Gen. 14:7). But this reference is best interpreted as Moses speaking of the land area that afterward would become known as the country of the Amalekites.

The Ammonites

The Ammonites came from Ammon, who had been born as a result of an incestuous relation between Lot and his younger daughter (Gen. 19:33–38). These peoples were, therefore, related to Israel. They lived east of the Jordan River, between the rivers Jabbok and Arnon (see map "Israel's Near Neighbors," page 101), until they were pushed farther east into the desert by Sihon, king of the Amorites.

Though related to Israel by ancestry, the Ammonites are invariably seen as hostile to them. Moses and the Israelites were careful to respect their land and to avoid taking anything that belonged to them, as Israel headed for the land of Canaan (Deut. 23:3–4).

The Ammonites oppressed Israel in the days of the judges (Judg. 10:7; 11:4–11) and were a problem to Israel in the time of the monarchy (1 Sam. 11:1–13; 2 Sam. 10:1–19) and the years after the monarchy (Jer. 40:14; 41:10; Neh. 4:3). Because of their wickedness, judgment was pronounced on them, and they have now disappeared from the earth (1 Kings 11:5, 7, 33; Ezek. 25:5; Zeph. 2:9).

The Assyrians

The Assyrians were Semites (descendants of Noah's son Shem). The bloodline and language of the Assyrians was originally quite close to that of the Babylonians. As the cen

The Amalekites settled in the desert southwest of the Dead Sea and down into the Sinai Peninsula.

turies went by, however, the Assyrians intermarried with other peoples very little, thus keeping some purity in their bloodline. These people originally settled in northern Mesopotamia on the Tigris River (see map "Israel's Distant Neighbors," page 103).

The Assyrians were one of several nations used by the Lord to discipline His people Israel. It must be remembered, however, in reading Israel's history that none of these foreign nations could have become strong enough to conquer Israel's covenanted land area except by Divine permission and because of Israel's sin (Lev. 26:23–33).

The Assyrians began to build an empire around 1100 B.C. (the era of the monarchy in Israel began in 1043 B.C.). But for about

two centuries the empire lay dormant. When King Ashurnasirpal II (883–859 B.C.) rose to power, he created a great Assyrian fighting machine and began conquering many areas. His son, Shalmaneser III (858–824 B.C.), inherited his father's war machine and conducted numerous campaigns against Syria and Palestine. Assyria then declined somewhat until the coming of Tiglath-pileser III (745–727 B.C.), a mighty warrior and able statesman, who brought Assyria to a place of great power and glory. He overran Israel and took tribute from King Menahem of Israel (cf. 2 Kings 15:19) and also took some of the conquered peoples to distant sections of his empire. Hoshea of Israel attempted to revolt against

Nations related to Israel

Terah

Haran — Nahor — Abraham

Lot

ISHMAEL
(by Hagar)

Isaac
(by Sarah)

MIDIAN
(by Keturah)

MOAB
(by oldest
daughter)

AMMON
(by youngest
daughter)

Esau-**EDOM**
(by Rebekah)

AMALEK
(grandson of Esau)

Assyria and felt the crushing blow of Assyrian power. Shalmaneser V (726–722 B.C.) succeeded his father and besieged Israel's capital city of Samaria for three years (2 Kings 17:3–6). The next Assyrian king, Sargon II, finished the job of defeating Israel and taking captive the Northern Kingdom.

Under the kings that followed, Assyria's stranglehold on the ancient world began to ease. With the exception of one or two kings, the remaining Assyrian kings did not distinguish themselves. The capital city of Assyria, Nineveh, fell in 612 B.C. After experiencing defeats at Haran (609 B.C.) and Carchemish (605 B.C.), the empire of Assyria was gone.

It should be noted also that God sent two of His prophets to speak to the Assyrians. Jonah brought his message in about 780 B.C., and later Nahum directed a word of judgment against them in 650 B.C.

The Babylonians

The ancient city of Babylon is known to us through the biblical record ("Babel" in Gen 10:10; 11:1–9). The city was eventually possessed by a semitic people. Babylon had an early period of strength (1800–1550 B.C.), but her most significant days of glory came about 600 B.C. and involved God's people.

As the power of Assyria began to wane, nations began to revolt successfully. In 626 B.C., Babylonia gained full independence

Israel's Near Neighbors

Sidon

Damascus

Tyre

Dan

PHOENICIA

ARAM (SYRIA)

Hazor

GESHUR

Acco

Sea of Chinnereth

Dor   Megiddo   Shunem

Taanach   Beth-shan   Ramoth-gilead

ISRAEL

Shechem

Penuel

AMMON

Shiloh

Aijalon   Bethel

Jordan

Rabbath-bene-ammon

Gezer   Gibeon

Gath   Jerusalem

Jerusalem

AMORITES

Gaza

JUDAH   Hebron

Salt Sea

Arad   Rabbah

Beersheba

AMALEK   Kir-moab

MOAB

Tamar

GREAT SEA

PHILISTIA

Kadesh-barnea

EDOM

EGYPT

◎ Capital
— International border

0   25   50   75 km

0   15   30   45 miles

from Assyria through the leadership of Nabopolasar. In 605 B.C., Nabopolasar (now in poor health) sent his son, Nebuchadnezzar, to fight the remnant of the Assyrian empire, which had been joined by the Egyptians under Pharaoh Neco II. In the battle of Carchemish, Nebuchadnezzar completely defeated the Assyrians and the Egyptians and established Babylon as the most powerful nation in the ancient Near East. Nebuchadnezzar pursued the Egyptians as they fled home to Egypt. But he stopped at Jerusalem and subjugated the Southern Kingdom of Judah. While there, he received word that his father had died, so he hurried back to Babylon to claim the throne (taking some Jews, like Daniel, with him as captives). In 568 B.C. he defeated Egypt, thus making complete his world conquests. He died in 562 B.C. None of his successors had his abilities. They were unable to keep this massive empire together for long. The kingdom of Babylon ended in the year 539 B.C., being taken over by the Medes and the Persians. But Babylon was raised up long enough to accomplish the purposes of God.

The Edomites

The Edomites were the descendants of Esau, the brother of Jacob. They settled south of the Dead Sea (Gen. 25:30; 36:1–9, 31–43). In the Bible, the Edomites are also called "Seir" or "Mount Seir" after the geographic area where they settled (Gen. 36:9; Ezek. 35:1–15).

Esau's hatred for his brother, Jacob, seemed to continue through his descendants. Being a near relative apparently made no difference to them. The Edomites refused to allow Moses and the Israelites passage through their land, thus causing great discomfort for Israel (Num. 20:18–21). For some 400 years nothing is mentioned about the Edomites. But they reappear during the monarchy period as an adversary of Israel (e.g., 1 Sam. 14:47; 2 Sam. 8:13–14; 1 Kings 11:15–16; 2 Chron. 20:22; 21:8; 25:11–12; 28:17). Because of their terrible treatment of "brother Jacob," the Edomites were severely denounced by the prophets (e.g., Obadiah; Isa. 34:5–8; Jer. 49:17; Amos 1:11–12).

The Egyptians

In many ways the most important foreign nation Israel dealt with was Egypt. The great importance of Egypt has been discussed in Genesis and Exodus (the first two foundational books). Egypt was used by God as the great protector of the infant nation of Israel (Gen. 42–50). Later Egypt became the great persecutor of Israel, thus bringing about the awesome display of God's power (Ex. 5–14). After the Exodus from Egypt, the nation of Egypt still affected Israel and Israel's foreign policy in the following centuries.

During the Old Testament times following the Exodus (1445–400 B.C.), Egypt never became a world power like Assyria and Babylon. They were, however, on several occasions a "thorn in the side" of the world powers. They joined with other nations to resist the Assyrians, then the Babylonians, and later on the Persians. On some occasions their actions directly affected Israel (e.g., 2 Kings 23:29, the killing of King Josiah).

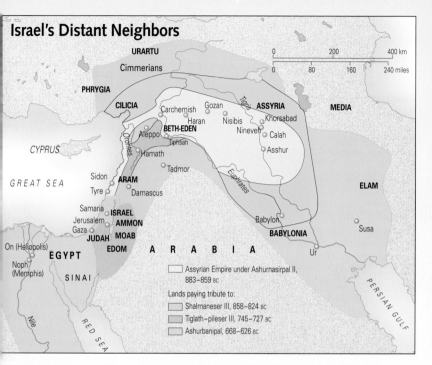

Israel's Distant Neighbors

URARTU

Cimmerians

PHRYGIA

CILICIA

Carchemish Gozan **ASSYRIA** **MEDIA**

Haran Nisibis Khorsabad

BETH-EDEN Nineveh

Aleppo Calah

CYPRUS Tiphsah

Asshur

Hamath

Tadmor

Sidon **ARAM**

GREAT SEA **ELAM**

Tyre Damascus

Samaria **ISRAEL**

Jerusalem **AMMON** Babylon

Gaza **MOAB** Susa

JUDAH **BABYLONIA**

On (Heliopolis) EDOM A R A B I A Ur

Noph **EGYPT**

(Memphis) SINAI

PERSIAN GULF

RED SEA

Nile

0 ____ 200 ____ 400 km

0 __ 80 __ 160 __ 240 miles

Tigris

Orontes

Euphrates

☐ Assyrian Empire under Ashurnasirpal II,
883–859 BC

Lands paying tribute to:

☐ Shalmaneser III, 858–824 BC

☐ Tiglath-pileser III, 745–727 BC

☐ Ashurbanipal, 668–626 BC

The Medo-Persians

Medo-Persia was a dual nation that dominated the ancient world from 539–330 B.C. It was composed of two similar peoples, the Medes and the Persians.

Media came under the rule of the Assyrians, as Assyrian documents testify. But Media began to rise to power, and in 614 B.C. they conquered the Assyrian city of Asshur. They then joined forces with the Babylonians to overthrow Nineveh in 612 B.C. Nebuchadnezzar of Babylon married the daughter of Cyaxares, the Median king,

thus strengthening the alliance between those two nations.

The Persians came into the area east of the Tigris River about 1500 B.C. For most of the following centuries they were dominated by the Medes. However, with the rise of Cyrus II in 550 B.C., Persia subdued Media. Media remained an important province, which is seen in the use of the dual name "Medes and Persians" (e.g., Dan. 5:28; Esther 1:19). This great empire was able to last for more than two centuries until it finally fell before Alexander the Great.

The Midianites

After the death of Sarah, Abraham married Keturah and had six sons by her (Gen. 25:1–6). The fourth of these sons was Midian. In order to insure that Isaac alone would be the "covenant" son, Midian and his brothers were given gifts and sent to the east. The Midianites were found in an area south and east of Palestine.

The Midianites do not appear often in Scripture. They are the ones who took Joseph to Egypt and sold him (Gen. 37:13–28). Exodus 2:15–22 records that Moses fled to the land of Midian after killing an Egyptian and there married a Midianite girl. The Midianites figure in the story of Balaam and the resistance to Israel as they prepared to enter Canaan (Num. 25:6–17; 31:1–8; Josh. 13:21). And the Midianites were one of the nations that oppressed Israel during the time of the judges. Gideon brought Israel deliverance from the Midianites (Judg. 6:33; 7:1–14, 25).

In the Genesis narrative the terms *Midianite* and *Ishmaelite* are used interchangeably. Most likely this is because they became closely associated through intermarriage. It should be noted that with these nomadic peoples racial lines were not rigidly adhered to, and so some very close connections can be observed on occasion.

The Moabites

Moab was a son of Lot, resulting from Lot's incestuous relationship with his older daughter (Gen. 19:33–37). The Moabites lived on the eastern side of the Dead Sea, below the Arnon River.

Moab's relationship with Israel was evidently not quite as hostile as some other nations. They seemed to be a more peaceful people. Moab, however, did refuse passage to the Israelites, but showed no hostile action when Israel went along their border in order to arrive on the east side of the Jordan (Judg. 11:17, 25–26; Deut. 23:3–4). The Moabites lived in peace with Israel for three hundred years (Judg. 11:25–26). Over the centuries there were, however, times of war. The Moabites oppressed Israel in the days of the judges (Judg. 3:12–30) and were themselves defeated by Saul (1 Sam. 14:47) and David (2 Sam. 8:2). Moab at times paid tribute to Israel (e.g., 2 Kings 3:4–5), but at other times was independent and prosperous. Several Israelite prophets warned Moab of coming judgment (e.g., Isa. 15; 16; Jer. 48).

The Philistines

Unlike many of Israel's neighbors, the Philistines were genetically and culturally unrelated. According to the Scriptures, they came from a place called Caphtor (Jer. 47:4; Amos 9:7), which is apparently a reference to the island of Crete. Archaeology would suggest a broader geographic origin for the Philistines. They not only came from Crete, but probably from numerous islands of the Aegean Sea and perhaps coastlands as well. About 1200 B.C. the Philistines attempted to invade the delta region of Egypt. Unable to defeat the armies of Pharaoh Rameses III, they settled on the southwest coast of Palestine.

The Philistines established a city-state type of organization. There were five major cities (Gath, Gaza, Ashkelon, Ashdod, and Ekron) which formed this powerful Philistine federation.

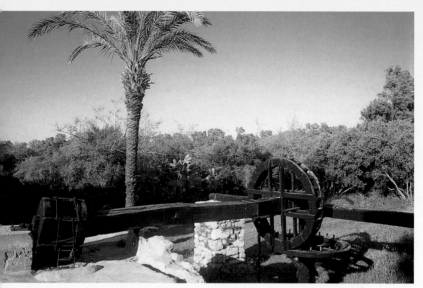

Mill at Ashkelon, one of the Philistines' major cities, situated on the Mediterranean coast.

The Philistines were a constant source of trouble for Israel. Philistine power was evidenced in Israel during the time of the judges (e.g., Judg. 14; 15; 1 Sam. 4). During the early days of Israel's monarchy, the Philistines played an important role. Saul had limited success, but David was able to subdue them (1 Sam. 13; 31; 2 Sam. 5). They were a problem for the kings of Israel at other times during the monarchy period. Their judgment was predicted by several of the prophets (e.g., Jer. 47:1–7; Ezek. 25:15–17). The Egyptians and Babylonians were able to crush the Philistines.

It should be noted that there are references to the Philistines' being in Palestine long before the 1200 B.C. date mentioned earlier (cf. Gen. 21:32, 34; 26:1; 26:8–16; Ex. 13:17; 23:31). It is most likely that these Philistines were tradesmen who settled along the coast of Palestine. They were probably part of a known migration of peoples from the Aegean area that took place many centuries before 1200 B.C. They were not the war-like peoples who were such a great problem to the Israelites in the days of the judges and the kings.

The Phoenicians

The Phoenicians were a racial mixture of Canaanites and Semites. The earliest settlers of the area were Canaanite, but they became overwhelmed by the great Semitic

The Sea Peoples

DORIAN GREEKS

Troy

HITTITES

ANATOLIA

Mycenae

Tarsus

Carchemish

Rhodes

Caphtor (Crete)

Ugarit

Elishah (Cyprus)

AMURRU

GREAT SEA

Sidon   Damascus

CANAAN

Ashkelon

Gaza

Movements of the Sea Peoples, c. 1250–1150 BCE

0   150   300 km
0   60   120   180 miles

EGYPT   Pi-Rameses (Rameses)

empires of the Fertile Crescent. The Phoenicians were one result of the intermixing of these racial groups. They occupied the coastal regions between the Lebanon Mountains and the Mediterranean Sea north of the city of Acco. Tyre and Sidon were the two most famous Phoenician cities.

The Phoenicians were not hostile toward Israel and did not seem to have the interest or the capacity to invade Israel. They were a commercially oriented people. With their two great seaports of Tyre and Sidon (and others) and with the availability of timber

for shipbuilding, they became world famous for their commercial activities.

The Old Testament Scriptures do not use the term "Phoenicia" but speak instead of the principle cities of Tyre and Sidon (e.g., 2 Sam. 5:11; 24:7; 1 Kings 7:14; Isa. 23:17; Jer. 47:4; Judg. 1:31; 1 Kings 17:9; 16:31). Where there were contacts with these people, the relationship seemed good.

The Syrians

The first settlers of the region commonly called Syria were evidently of Hamitic descent (cf. Gen. 10:6–20). These

Canaanites were eventually invaded and taken over by a Semitic race, the Arameans. The tribes who lived in this region were not united in the early days of Old Testament history and, therefore, were not a significant political or military force. The ancient city of Damascus was the main city of this area.

The first hostile activity with Israel came in the days of King David as he extended the borders of Israel (2 Sam. 8:3–13). David was repeatedly successful against the Syrians (2 Sam. 10:6–19). But after the division of Israel's kingdom (931 B.C.), the Syrians enjoyed their period of greatest power (from about 900 to 730 B.C.). During those years they were sometimes in alliance with Israel or Judah, whereas at other times they were vicious enemies (e.g., 1 Kings 15:18–20; 2 Kings 13:3–7). Syria acted as a natural buffer zone between Israel and the great powers of the north and east.

RUTH

This book complements Judges. The setting of Ruth is in the era of the judges (1:1). The book does not advance the history of Israel, but it does illustrate life in the days of the judges.

Important Data About Ruth

1. Key Words: Kinsman and redeemer (based on Lev. 25:25, 47–79; Deut. 25:5–6)
2. Key Chapter: 4—The family line of David
3. Key Verses: 1:15–16; 4:10
4. Key Characters: Ruth, Naomi, and Boaz
5. Meaning of "Ruth": Obviously the name of the central character of the book
6. Geography of Ruth: Tribal area of Benjamin and the country of Moab

INTRODUCTION TO RUTH

Authorship and Date of Ruth

The Jewish Talmud claims that Samuel wrote the book, but the author is unknown. It was not written prior to the time of David, since he is mentioned in 4:22. Since David is mentioned but David's son Solomon is not mentioned, it has led some to assume that it was written before Solomon's time. Samuel could have written the book. If he did, a date of about 1000 B.C. would be given.

Purpose of Ruth

One purpose of the book is to reveal that there were godly people during the era of the theocracy. Even though the nation found itself in deep apostasy, there were people in Israel who loved and obeyed the Lord God of Israel. In the book of Judges Israel forsakes the Lord and turns to idols, whereas in the book of Ruth one Gentile woman turns from her idols to serve the living and true God. Another purpose of the

Ruth

Basic Outline of Ruth

I. Ruth's Decision to Follow Naomi (chap. 1)

II. Ruth's Faithfulness to Naomi (chap. 2)

III. Ruth's Claim upon Boaz (chap. 3)

IV. Ruth's Redemption by Boaz (chap. 4)

"Shepherds' Fields", Bethlehem, where Ruth gleaned on a field belonging to her future husband Boaz.

book is to reveal something of the family line of Israel's greatest king, David.

Special Considerations on Ruth

The discussion under this same heading for Judges applies to Ruth as well. Leviticus 25:25 and 47–49 teach the concept of the "kinsman redeemer" that is important as background for the story of Ruth.

SUMMARY OF RUTH

Ruth's Decision to Follow Naomi (chap. 1)

The story begins by noting that famine had hit the land of Israel, which also indicates that the people were living in sin and disobedience (cf. Deut. 11:13–17). It also suggests that Israel was either in or heading into a time of foreign oppression. A family of Israel moved to Moab to try to avoid the famine. While in Moab the two sons married Moabite women, something expressly forbidden in the law (cf. Deut. 7:3; 23:3). Eventually the two sons died, as did the father, leaving three widows to face life alone. When news came that the famine was over (some judge had evidently delivered a repentant Israel), the mother, Naomi, decided to return home. Ruth, one of her daughters-in-law, insisted on going with her.

Ruth's Faithfulness to Naomi (chap. 2)

Ruth volunteered to care for the needs of Naomi by going into the fields and gleaning. Under the law (Lev. 19:9–10) the poor could enter fields, orchards, and vineyards and pick up leftover fruit or grain in order to provide food to meet their needs. It was a humbling task, but Ruth was willing to do it and in so doing put herself in the place for great blessing. Boaz was the owner of the field in which Ruth was gleaning. Boaz had heard of the godliness of Ruth (2:12 with Deut. 32:11) and her devotion to Naomi. He responded by allowing her to take home an unusual amount of grain (2:15–16, 19). Boaz's godliness and devotion to the Lord is seen in his obedience to the command to let people glean in his fields. (In light of the past famine, there would be a tendency to be grasping and to hoard all one could.)

Ruth's Claim upon Boaz (chap. 3)

To understand the story of Ruth, two customs of Israel must be kept in mind: (1) No land could be sold in perpetuity, that is, sold and kept forever by another. God did not want land falling into the hands of a few or passing to another tribe. (2) A male heir had to carry on the family line.

In the law a man was to be a "kinsman redeemer" when it was necessary to buy back the inheritance of a poor relative, or to buy back a person from slavery, or to build the family of a deceased relative.

Acting on Naomi's instructions, Ruth went to Boaz and claimed his protection, since he was a near relative of Naomi. Boaz was willing (and anxious) to do this, but there existed a relative who was closer to Naomi than he.

Ruth's Redemption by Boaz (chap. 4)

Going to the gate of the city (where public transactions were carried out), Boaz took the necessary legal steps to care for the matter. In the end, Boaz married Ruth, and they had a son whom they named Obed. Obed was the grandfather of David the king.

8.

1 Samuel

INTRODUCTION TO 1 SAMUEL

Authorship and Date of 1 Samuel

The books of 1 and 2 Samuel, originally one book, were divided into the present two books in the third century B.C. The Jewish Talmud states that Samuel wrote part of the book (1 Samuel 1– 24) and that Nathan and Gad composed the rest (cf. 1 Chronicles 29:29). The idea of there being several authors does not detract from the unity of the books or from the doctrine of inspiration.[1] For this study, a date of 975 B.C. is given for these books.

Purpose of 1 Samuel

First Samuel is given to record the great transition in the national life of Israel, as Israel left the theocracy and went into the monarchy. Samuel was the key individual during this time, and 1 Samuel provides the account of his ministry.

Special Considerations on 1 Samuel

The book begins with the birth of Samuel, which was about 1100 B.C., and ends with the death of Saul (1011 B.C.). This foundational book covers about ninety years.

1 Samuel

Basic Outline of 1 Samuel

I. Samuel: Judge and Prophet in Israel (chaps. 1–7)

II. Saul: The First King of Israel (chaps. 8–12)

III. The Decline of Saul and the Rise of David (chaps. 13–31)

Important Data About 1 Samuel

1. Key Word: King
2. Key Chapter: 8—The first king in Israel
3. Key Verses: 2:30; 8:7; 15:22–23; 16:7
4. Key Characters: Samuel, Saul, and David
5. Meaning of "1 Samuel": The first of two books named for the key figure of the early chapters
6. Geography of 1 Samuel: The land of Israel

SUMMARY OF 1 SAMUEL

Samuel: Judge and Prophet in Israel (chaps. 1–7)

The Birth of Samuel (1:1–2:10)
The significant role of Samuel in the history of Israel is often overlooked. He was born at a time when spiritually Israel was still in her descending spiral (Judg. 2:19); when Israel was weak and vulnerable before her enemies (1 Sam. 4:1–11); and when the voice of God was rarely heard in the land (3:1). Samuel was the last of the judges (7:6, 15); was a priest of God (1:1; 16:5 with 1 Chron. 6:33–36); and was the first notable prophet of God since Moses (3:19–21). From the human perspective, it was Samuel who changed Israel from a weak, idolatrous people to a nation spiritually alive and strong for the Lord God.

Samuel was born into the home of a Levite named Elkanah. (Note that they lived in the tribal area of Ephraim and were therefore called Ephraimites, but they were of the tribe of Levi.) Elkanah the Levite had two wives, which may suggest a low moral condition in Israel at that time. One wife was named Hannah, and she had no children. There was bitter antagonism between the two wives, much of which came from the fact that Hannah was childless. Evidently it took Hannah many years before she humbled herself before the Lord

The "burial place" of the prophet Samuel.

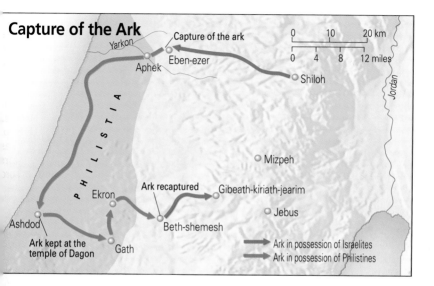

Capture of the Ark

Capture of the ark

Yarkon

Eben-ezer

Aphek

Shiloh

0   10   20 km

0   4   8   12 miles

Jordan

P H I L I S T I A

Mizpeh

Ekron

Ark recaptured

Gibeath-kiriath-jearim

Jebus

Ashdod

Beth-shemesh

Ark kept at the temple of Dagon

Gath

➡ Ark in possession of Israelites
➡ Ark in possession of Philistines

and prayed earnestly for a child (1:7, 10, 15). God honored her and gave her a son whom she named Samuel (1:27). She fulfilled the vow she had made and gave Samuel to the Lord for unique service in the Tabernacle (1:11, 28).

The Childhood of Samuel (2:11–3:21)

Samuel's environment at the Tabernacle had both positive and negative aspects to it. It was positive in that he was intimately involved with the high priest, Eli, and had the opportunity of serving God from his childhood. But it was negative in that he was exposed to Eli's two godless and immoral sons (2:11–12).

In those years it became clear to all in Israel that Samuel was uniquely God's man (3:19–4:1). God revealed an important life principle to Samuel in those early days— "those who honor Me I will honor" (2:30). This statement undoubtedly echoed in Samuel's thoughts all his life and was reflected in the life he lived.

The Ministry of Samuel (4:1–7:17)

Samuel was the key man in holding Israel together during the final, discouraging days of the theocracy. But even though some tragic events occurred (such as the military defeats at the hands of the Philistines and the capture of the Ark of the Covenant, 4:1–11), Samuel led the nation back to the Lord and into times of military victory (7:3–14). The majority of Samuel's significant ministry is summarized in just a few words (7:15–17).

Saul: The First King of Israel
(chaps. 8:1–12:25)

Israel's Demand for a King (8:1–22)

On several occasions in the era of the theocracy, the people of Israel had seriously considered the idea of having an earthly king rule over them (Judg. 8:22; 9:6). But the idea blossomed into reality when Samuel became quite old. It appeared to the elders of Israel that it was time to make the move to a monarchy (8:1–5). The matter was displeasing to Samuel and offensive to the Lord (8:6–7).

It must be noted that the idea of a king was within the plan of God (cf. Deut. 17:14–20). But on this occasion, the demand for a king was wrong for two basic reasons. First, the demand was premature. When God was ready to give them a king He would do so (David? the Messiah?). Second, the demand for a king was wrong because their attitude was wrong.

> Samuel's opposition . . . was a condemnation of the people's spirit and motives for requesting a king: they wished to be "like all the nations" in having a king (8:5, 20). It was also a tacit statement of disbelief in the power and presence of God: they wanted a king to go before them and fight their battles (v.20).[2]

The Lord offered Samuel comfort by telling him that the nation was not rejecting Samuel, but they were rejecting God Himself (8:7). This rejection of God's rulership climaxed here, but it had been going on throughout the period of the judges.

God granted Israel's request and gave them what they wanted but also warned them of what lay ahead in this new form of government.

> This change of government called for heavy taxation of the people. Under God's "best" form, there had been no need for taxes to support a civil government. There was no king or expensive court, no civil programs or authorities; the people could live tax-free. But this was radically changed when they received the monarchy. In this connection God's instruction to Samuel at the time of the people's request for a king is noteworthy. . . . God wanted the people to recognize the unique benefit they had been enjoying under His prescribed theocracy.[3]

Saul's Anointing and Recognition as King of Israel (9:1–12:25)

Evidently God gave Israel the kind of king they wanted (9:1–2) but did intend to use him in significant way (9:16). Samuel first anointed Saul as king privately (9:3–10:16) and later anointed him in a public ceremony (10:17–24).

> The oil of anointing, when used in worship, was a symbol of the divine Spirit; but in regal consecration it marked God's gift of His Spirit to aid the king of Israel in administering His rule. . . . This title of "the anointed one" . . . was only used absolutely of the king. Subsequently the word became the title for the great Davidite who was to come and to complete the expected kingdom of God. All together, the noun "anointed" occurs thirty-nine times in the OT. Twenty-three times it is the title for the reigning king of Israel.[4]

Although he was anointed as Israel's king, some doubted that he could really lead Israel (10:27). But Saul's credentials as king were firmly established when he led Israel to a great military victory at Jabesh-Gilead (11:1–15).

The settlement mound of the ancient Canaanite stronghold of Beth-shan, where Saul and Jonathan's bodies were displayed in triumph by the Philistines after their deaths at the disastrous Battle of Gilboa.

Period of the Kingdoms

1043 (1 Sam. 8)	931 (2 Kings 12)			(2 Kings 17) 721	(2 Kings 25) 586
UNITED	**DIVIDED**				**SINGLE**

KING SAUL	KING DAVID	KING SOLOMON	**ISRAEL**	TRIBES OF:	REUBEN
					SIMEON
					GAD
					ISSACHAR
					ZEBULUN
					MANASSEH
					EPHRAIM
					DAN
					ASHER
					NAPHTALI
			JUDAH		JUDAH
					BENJAMIN

After this great victory, which brought Saul general recognition as king, Samuel stepped down as the judge in Israel. He turned the civil authority over to Saul and exhorted Israel to fear and obey the Lord (12:1–25).

The Decline of Saul and the Rise of David (chaps. 13–31)

The remainder of 1 Samuel chronicles the willful disobedience of King Saul. His deliberate, disobedient choices were based on his ignorance of God and His Word as well as on the fact that he feared men more than he feared God.

The first step down in Saul's life was when he impatiently intruded into the priestly role and sacrificed animals. When confronted with his sin, he put the blame elsewhere. Like Moses', Saul's one act of public disobedience cost him a great deal. In Saul's case, he would lose his kingship (13:8–14). The second step down in Saul's decline occurred when he refused to completely obey God's clear command. God had a score to settle with the Amalekites, a score that dated back to the time of the Exodus (cf. 15:2 with Ex. 17:8–16 and Deut. 25:17–19). Saul was to completely destroy all the Amalekites and all of their livestock. His obedience was incomplete (15:8–9, 20–26). Saul tried to argue his case (15:20–21) but was met with a scathing denunciation from Samuel (15:22–23, 28). As far as God was concerned Saul was through as king, and the Spirit left Saul (16:14). A new king, David, was chosen by God and was anointed in private by Samuel (16:1, 13). The emphasis of 1 Samuel now shifts away from Saul and toward David.

David's name became well-known in Israel after his amazing victory over the Philistine giant Goliath (17:1–52). More military successes came to David after that event. David received the praise of the people ("Saul has slain his thousands and David his ten thousands," 18:7) but also the resentment and violence of Saul (18:8–11). Although Saul soon came to understand that David was God's choice as Israel's next king, he repeatedly tried to kill David. This willful refusal to submit to God's will was the third step down in the unhappy decline of Saul.

The final step in Saul's decline was his involvement with the witch of En-dor (28:1–21). After the death of Samuel (25:1), it became clear to Saul that God had ceased all communication with him (28:6). When faced with another invasion by the Philistines, Saul was frightened and sought the Lord. When God failed to answer him, Saul entered the realm of the occult (cf. Deut. 18:9–11). A man with so much potential and with such a notable start ended up so poorly. The very next day Saul died on the battlefield. It was an unnecessary and tragic end, but the inevitable end of one who does not know and reverence God.

9.
2 Samuel

INTRODUCTION TO 2 SAMUEL

Authorship and Date of 2 Samuel

See the introduction to 1 Samuel for the discussion of authorship and date of this book.

Important Data About 2 Samuel

1. Key Word: David
2. Key Chapter: 7—The great Davidic Covenant
3. Key Verses: 7:8–16; 12:7–14
4. Key Characters: David, Nathan, Abner, Joab, and Absalom
5. Meaning of "2 Samuel": The second of two books named for the key figure of the early chapters of the first book
6. Geography of 2 Samuel: The land of Judah and Israel

Purpose of 2 Samuel

The purpose of 2 Samuel is to continue the account of the development of the monarchy in Israel. Second Samuel is the record of the reign of David, Israel's greatest king. The book also sets forth the elements of the Davidic Covenant.

Basic Outline of 2 Samuel

2 Samuel

I. David's Rule over Judah (chaps. 1–4)

II. David's Rule over All Israel (chaps. 5–24)

This area of Jerusalem was where the Jebusite city, captured by David, originally stood.

Special Considerations on 2 Samuel

The book of 2 Samuel records the years when David actually sat on the throne as king. His reign lasted for forty years (1011–971 B.C.).

SUMMARY OF 2 SAMUEL

David's Rule over Judah (chaps. 1–4)

The Lamentation of David (1)

The book of 1 Samuel concludes with Saul's committing suicide on the battlefield after being wounded by the Philistines. The book of 2 Samuel begins with David's being informed about the deaths of Saul and his sons by an Amalekite, who was probably a mercenary sol-dier in Saul's army. The man claimed he had killed the nearly dead Saul, at Saul's request. Since the Scriptures indicate that Saul had indeed died by his own hand (1 Sam. 31:4–6), we know the man lied. No doubt he was hoping to be rewarded for eliminating David's enemy and removing the last obstacle to the throne. But David, who had himself repeatedly refused to kill Saul ("the Lord's anointed"), looked with anger on the Amalekite and had him executed, condemned by his own testimony (1:16).

Instead of rejoicing over the death of Saul and his sons, David grieved (1:17–27). His sorrow was particularly great for his close friend Jonathan.

The Crowning of David and the Years of Civil War (2–4)

David had the right to the throne at Saul's death, since he had been chosen and anointed by Samuel, God's prophet-priest. But only the tribe of Judah was willing to anoint David and recognize him as king (2:4). Most likely tribal jealousies, which emerged from time to time in Israel's history, kept the other tribes from immediately joining in. Instead Ish-bosheth, a son of Saul, was made king over the northern area. He was supported by a mighty man by the name of Abner. This two-kingdom situation lasted for seven years. During that time wars were fought between the two nations. As time went on, however, it became clear that the kingdom of David was prospering and Ish-bosheth's kingdom was declining (3:1). When the mighty Abner was murdered (3:30) and King Ish-bosheth was assassinated (4:5–6), the northern tribes realized that they needed to unite under David.

David's Rule over All Israel (chaps. 5–24)

David's Early Reign in Power and Prosperity (5–10)

The leaders of the North recognized that it was not wise to be a divided people. They knew that David had been anointed to be king over all of Israel. They knew that David had played an important part in the recent military history of the North as well as the South. These truths plus the realization that they all had a common heritage brought the two groups together (5:1–3). Tens of thousands gathered in a great celebration at Hebron and made David king over all Israel (cf. 1 Chron. 12:23–40).

Several significant steps were taken immediately by David. First, he defeated Jerusalem and made it the political capital of the nation (5:6–10). David had been ruling from Hebron located in the South. This move made Israel's capital more centrally located and

Davidic Covenant

1. David's name will be great	This was fulfilled in David's own lifetime, as well as throughout history.
2. David would have rest	Rest from his enemies was one of the realities of David's life.
3. David would have a house	This does not refer to a physical structure but rather a ruling dynasty. His line would never be cut off.
4. David would have a throne	The right to rule Israel would always belong to David's line.
5. David would have a Kingdom	This included an actual land area to rule over, as well as the other aspects of a kingdom.

(**Note:** *Numbers 3,4, and 5 await ultimate fulfillment in Jesus Christ.*)

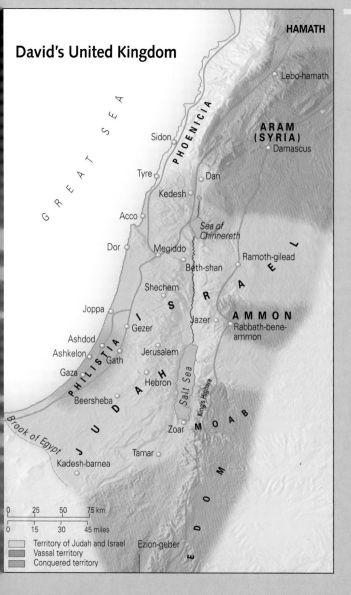

David's United Kingdom

HAMATH

Lebo-hamath

GREAT SEA

PHOENICIA

ARAM (SYRIA)

Sidon

Damascus

Tyre

Dan

Kedesh

Acco

Sea of Chinnereth

Dor

Megiddo

Beth-shan

Ramoth-gilead

Shechem

I S R A E L

Joppa

Jazer

AMMON

Gezer

Rabbath-bene-ammon

Ashdod

Ashkelon

Jerusalem

PHILISTIA

Gath

J U D A H

Gaza

Hebron

Salt Sea

King's Highway

Beersheba

M O A B

Brook of Egypt

Zoar

Tamar

E D O M

Kadesh-barnea

0	25	50	75 km
0	15	30	45 miles

Ezion-geber

Territory of Judah and Israel
Vassal territory
Conquered territory

more defensible. Second, he brought the Tabernacle to Jerusalem, thus making Jerusalem the religious capital of Israel also (6:12–19).

David was a capable military man who also sensed his need to depend on the Lord God. As a result, David won battle after battle, destroying enemy after enemy. In so doing, David expanded and secured the borders of Israel (5:17–25; 8:1–18; 10:1– 19). David aggressively pushed the borders of Israel toward the boundaries granted under the Palestinian Covenant. Militarily David and Saul stand in sharp contrast. Saul's battles were primarily defensive, reacting to the hostile actions of some nation. David also responded to hostile nations, but David's battles were far more offensive in nature.

During a time of rest from war, David observed how beautiful his own house was in comparison to the Tabernacle, God's house. David's house was constructed out of expensive cedar wood, whereas God's house was a tent made out of cloth (7:1). To his friend and counselor Nathan the prophet, David expressed his desire to build a beautiful, permanent temple for the Lord. Nathan approved of the project but later that night was informed by God that since David was a man of war and bloodshed, he was not to build the Temple (7:5; 1 Chron. 22:8). But God responded to the heart desire of His servant David by entering into an eternal, unconditional covenant with him. The Davidic Covenant is a subdivision of the Abrahamic Covenant and develops further the promise of a nation and a king. Second Samuel 7 is the central passage on the Davidic Covenant, but many other Scriptures speak of it, including 1 Chronicles 17:11–27; Psalm 89; Jeremiah 33:14–22; Ezekiel 37:24–25; 2 Samuel 23:1– 7; and Luke 1:32–33.

Since the Davidic Covenant looks ahead to David's greater Son, Jesus Christ, there are some clear prophetic implications to this covenant. They are (1) Israel must be preserved as a nation and eventually returned to the land of Palestine; (2) David's Son, Jesus the Messiah, must return to rule over the covenanted kingdom; and (3) a literal, earthly kingdom for the nation of Israel must be instituted, over which Christ will reign.[1]

David's Later Reign of Sin and Trouble (11–24)

Often in times of great success and victory, when all seems well, defeat is experienced. So it was in the case of the great and victorious King David, when he committed adultery with Bathsheba (11:1–4). The sequence of sin was common—he saw, he inquired, and then he participated. His taking of another man's wife was bad enough, but the situation got worse because sin was not confessed. When David learned that Bathsheba was pregnant (11:5), he initiated a series of cover-ups, which finally ended in the death (actually murder) of Uriah, the unsuspecting husband of Bathsheba. David, therefore, was guilty of both murder and adultery. Both of these sins were capital crimes in Israel, and there was no sacrifice available to cover them. David the king faced death, but though burdened by terrible guilt (cf. Ps. 32:3–4), he would not confess. It took a story and declaration by his friend Nathan to bring David to the point of genuine confession (cf. Ps. 51). God extended mercy toward David.

David purchased the site for the Temple from Araunah. The Dome of the Rock now stands there.

His sin was forgiven, but Nathan informed David that there would be two results of his sin: (1) the baby born to Bathsheba from their union would die, and (2) David would see and experience sin and rebellion in his own house for the rest of his life. And so it happened: one son raped one of his daughters; one son murdered another son; and one ran away from home only to foment a national rebellion when he returned (13:1–18:33). David's sins of murder and adultery had been forgiven, but even forgiven sin has its consequences. This spiritual and moral failure of King David has been recorded as a warning to all.

David did fail on a number of occasions, but he was still a "man after God's own heart." He dealt with his sin and drew upon the power and grace of God to live with the consequences of sin.

10.
1 Kings

INTRODUCTION TO 1 KINGS

Authorship and Date of 1 Kings

The two books of 1 and 2 Kings were originally one book, and the author is unknown.

Important Data About 1 Kings

1. Key Word: Division
2. Key Chapter: 12—The dividing of the kingdom
3. Key Verses: 8:22–26; 12:16
4. Key Characters: Solomon, Rehoboam, Jeroboam, Ahab, Jezebel, Elijah, Asa, and Jehoshaphat
5. Meaning of "1 Kings": The first of two books named after the kings of Israel and Judah from Solomon to the Babylonian captivity whose histories they record
6. Geography of 1 Kings: The land of Judah and Israel

It is generally agreed by commentators that the content of 1 and 2 Kings was compiled before the captivity of Judah, with the final editing taking place in the captivity period. Some believe that the author was a Jewish captive living in Babylon, whereas others point to the prophet Jeremiah as the most likely candidate. In either case, the date of writing would be about 600–575 B.C.

Basic Outline of 1 Kings

1 Kings

I. The Reign of Solomon over the United Kingdom (chaps. 1–11)

II. The Early Days of the Divided Kingdom (chaps. 12–22)

Authentic scale model of Solomon's Temple

Purpose of 1 Kings

First Kings was written to continue the story of the united monarchy under David's son Solomon. It was also written to record the division of the kingdom into North and South. The book is not just a view of historical events but a commentary on the great spiritual issues that brought about those events.

Special Considerations on 1 Kings

The book begins with Solomon's coming to the throne and ruling all of Israel, and it ends with Jehoshaphat's reigning in Judah and Ahaziah's ruling in Israel. This would, therefore, cover a period of about 125 years.

SUMMARY OF 1 KINGS

The Reign of Solomon over the United Kingdom (chaps. 1–11)

Solomon's Accession to the Throne (1:1–2:11)

As David neared the age of seventy (2 Sam. 5:4) and was weak and infirm, it became clear to all in Israel that a new king would be coming to the throne. David had evidently made a fundamental error by not clearly and publicly declaring which son would be his successor. Privately, David had promised Bathsheba that her son Solomon would be the next king (1:16–17). But in the absence of a clear, public statement, David's fourth son Adonijah (probably David's oldest living son) attempted to take the throne for himself (1:5, 18–19). This attempt was thwarted when David ordered Nathan the prophet, Zadok the priest, and other key individuals to publicly anoint and proclaim Solomon as king (1:32–40). Considering the potential for chaos and unrest, the transition of the throne to Solomon went fairly smoothly. After giving the new king some good advice, Israel's greatest king, David, died (2:1–11).

Solomon's Establishment of the Kingdom (2:12–5:18)

After removing several of his adversaries (2:12–46), Solomon put together a highly organized empire. He made numerous political alliances, engaged in many building projects, fortified the defenses of Israel, and developed a complex bureaucracy.

Solomon's wisdom (given him by God, 3:4–12) became well known throughout the region (4:29–34). David's military victories, Solomon's wisdom, and God's obvious favor made it possible for all Israel to live in peace and prosperity (4:25).

Solomon's Building Program (6:1–10:29)

David had desired to build a house for God, but it was his son Solomon who actually built the Temple in Jerusalem. It took about seven years to build this multimillion-dollar structure. With its abundance of gold, silver, marble, and fine woods, the Temple was one of the wonders of the world.

The high point in Israel's history in the Old Testament was perhaps the dedication of this Temple. Never again do we find the nation, as a whole, living in such peace and prosperity

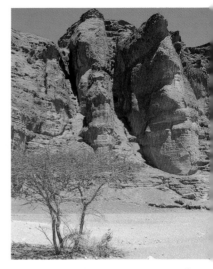

Solomon operated copper mines at Timna, far to the south, near the Red Sea.

and apparently so completely devoted to the Lord. Both king and people were united in obedience to the law of God. Solomon's marvelous prayer on that great day of dedication gives a fitting illustration of those prosperous days in Israel (cf. 8:1, 22–25, 54–56).

Solomon's Spiritual Failure and End as Israel's King (11:1–43)

Two Scriptures mentioned previously have great import in the following events. In 1 Samuel 8, God had warned Israel that heavy taxation would accompany the monarchy. In order to maintain his huge government, luxurious lifestyle, and numerous building projects, Solomon turned more and more to the taxation of his people. This tax burden caused

Solomon's United Kingdom

Damascus

Tyre

Dan

**ARAM
(SYRIA)**

PHOENICIA

Asher

Naphtali

Hazor

GESHUR

GREAT SEA

Acco

Cabul

*Sea of
Chinnereth*

BASHAN

Zebulun

Megiddo

Dor

NAPHATH
DOR

Issachar

Jezreel

Ramoth-
gilead

Taanach

Beth-shan

Hepher

ISRAEL

Socoh

Shechem

Succoth

Mahanaim

GILEAD

Joppa

Shiloh

Rabbath-bene-
ammon

Ephraim

Beth-horon

Baalath

Gezer

Gibeon

AMMON

Shaalbim

Benjamin

Jericho

Jerusalem

PHILISTIA

Gath

Beth-shemesh

GAD

Gaza

JUDAH

Hebron

Salt Sea

Beersheba

MOAB

Tamar

Brook of Egypt

EDOM

United kingdom of Israel and Judah
Vassal kingdoms
Boundary of Solomon's empire
Boundary of administrative district
Solomonic fortification or building project

0		25		50 km
0	10	20	30 miles

Ezion-geber

Kings of Judah and Israel in 1 Kings (15; 22:40–53)

JUDAH

Abijam
He reigned for just three years. He was not totally devoted to the Lord.

Asa
He was a godly king who ruled for forty-one years. He destroyed the places of idolatry in the Southern Kingdom.

Jehoshaphat
He was a good king who obeyed the Lord. He reigned for twenty-five years and made peace with the North. Kings of Israel in 1 Kings (15:25–22:40, 51–53).

ISRAEL

Nadab
He was evil like his father, Jeroboam. He was on the throne for just two years.

Baasha
He was a sinful king who ruled twenty-four years after completely destroying everyone in the family of Nadab.

Elah
He continued the sins and the policies of Baasha, his father, during his two years on the throne.

Zimri
He was a powerful general in the army who assassinated Elah and all of his family. He ruled for only seven days.

Omri
He was another leader in the army who came to power after killing Zimri. He was forced to rule alongside another claimant to the throne, Tibni. For three years these two ruled as kings in the North, until Omri finally won out. Omri made some effective long-range plans for Israel, such as moving Israel's capital to Samaria and strengthening Israel through alliances. One such alliance brought the evil Jezebel to Israel.

Ahab
Ruling for twenty-two years, along with his wife Jezebel, he brought Israel to its lowest spiritual level. Baalism became the religion of the Northern Kingdom, and the Scriptures declare that Ahab and Jezebel were the most wicked rulers in the entire history of the North (16:30–31; 21:25). In order to deal with this extreme crisis, God raised up the fiery prophet Elijah. Elijah was used to counter the evils of Baalism and call some in Israel back to the Lord.

Ahaziah
This son of Ahab and Jezebel was wicked like his parents. Fortunately, he ruled for only two years.

High Place, Dan. Jeroboam placed a golden calf at Dan, in the northern part of his kingdom.

deep unrest and became terribly oppressive (as the cries of the people later on indicate, 12:4). In Deuteronomy 17, God had warned kings not to multiply horses, silver, and wives. The horse was the basis of military might, but God wanted Israel to trust *Him*. Silver, and all other forms of wealth, would breed independence from God. Many wives (often part of treaties made with foreign kings) would bring their idols with them and in the process turn the king's devotion away from the Lord. Solomon flagrantly violated all three of these prohibitions (cf. 1 Kings 10:26; 2 Chron. 9:25; 1 Kings 10:14, 27; 11:1–5).

In his glory years Solomon did not act wisely, failing to remember that even kings are subject to the "constitution." He antagonized his subjects and offended the Holy One of Israel. His devotion to the many idols of his wives brought a word of judgment from God (11:11–13). As a result of his sin, the kingdom would be divided. Solomon's son would be king over but two tribes. Only the existence of the Davidic Covenant kept Solomon's line from being cut off.

The rest of Solomon's life is passed over quickly in the text of Scripture. The author of 1 Kings now introduces Jeroboam, who will become a central figure in the monarchy period. Jeroboam, a servant of Solomon, will become the first king of the Northern Kingdom (11:26–31).

The Early Days of the Divided Kingdom (chaps. 12–22)

The Division of the Kingdom (12:1–20)
Solomon did not make David's error of failing

to unmistakably set apart his successor. His son Rehoboam was made king. After Solomon's death, Rehoboam went to Shechem in north central Israel to be formally crowned as the fourth king of the united kingdom. However, it was at that time that the people demanded relief from the heavy taxation of Solomon as a prerequisite for their uniting under the kingship of Rehoboam (12:1–4). Rehoboam foolishly refused this legitimate request with the result that the northern tribes refused to acknowledge Rehoboam as king (12:13–16). Instead they made Jeroboam of Ephraim their king (12:20).

Although Rehoboam's lack of wisdom brought about the division of the kingdom, it was not the cause of it. There were several reasons for the breakup of the kingdom of Israel. First and foremost was the spiritual defection of Solomon.

> Solomon's sin struck at the heart of the theocracy; to follow other gods in any sense was to deny the covenant with Yahweh and make the new temple a farce.[1]

This by itself would have brought about God's judgment. But a second reason for division can be found in a long-standing tribal jealousy that was promoted by Judah's being the preeminent kingly tribe. Solomon deepened this jealousy by taxing all the tribes but Judah, by concentrating his building projects in Judah, and by emphasizing the defense of Judah. His harsh treatment of certain northerners, by offering to give away their cities to another king (9:10–13), added to the already existing

rivalry and antagonism.[2] And a third reason for the division can be found in Solomon's exploitation of the people.

> Solomon's personal pride and selfishness certainly contributed to the problem. . . . His vast building operations, though improving his power and prestige, did little to help his own people. . . . The people soon realized that they were being sacrificed for personal enrichment rather than for national welfare. . . . Unrest continued to increase.[3]

In light of these powerful forces already at work, the blame for the division belongs to Solomon and not Rehoboam. But division came and would continue for the next 210 years.

The year of the division was 931 B.C. The histories of the two kingdoms are interwoven in the Scripture text until the captivity of the Northern Kingdom in 721 B.C. (2 Kings 17). During those years the two kingdoms were often friendly and cooperative with one another, but at other times they were at war.

Rehoboam of Judah and Jeroboam of Israel (12:21–14:31)

Although political division had taken place, the two nations were still united religiously. Jerusalem, in the south, was still the center of Israel's worship and religious activity. Jeroboam reasoned that he would not be able to maintain the political division while religious unity existed (12:26–27). Therefore, he chose to alter the religion of the North just enough to deprive Jerusalem of its role as the only center of a unified worship of the Lord. Jeroboam made two golden calves (bulls) and placed one

The Kingdoms of Israel and Judah

Sidon

Damascus

Tyre

Dan

PHOENICIA

ARAM (SYRIA)

Hazor

GESHUR

Acco

Sea of Chinnereth

Dor

Megiddo

Shunem

Taanach

Beth-shan

Ramoth-gilead

I S R A E L

Shechem

Shiloh

Penuel

AMMON

Aijalon

Bethel

Rabbath-bene-ammon

Gezer

Gibeon

Jordan

Gath

Jerusalem

Gaza

AMORITES

J U D A H

Hebron

Salt Sea

Arad

Rabbah

Beersheba

A M A L E K

Kir-moab

M O A B

G R E A T   S E A

P H I L I S T I A

Tamar

Kadesh-barnea

E G Y P T

E D O M

○ Capital

·–·– International border

| 0 | 25 | 50 | 75 km |
| 0 | 15 | 30 | 45 miles |

in the northern part of his kingdom at Dan, and the other in the southern part of his kingdom at Bethel. Jeroboam was not introducing new gods. Rather, he was claiming that these calves were visible representations of the Lord who "brought them up from the land of Egypt" (12:28). He was not saying that the Lord was the calf. The calf, or bull, was revered in ancient times as a symbol of great strength. And, too, Jeroboam had history on his side. He could point to Israel's first high priest, Aaron, who once made a calf of gold for worship. Jeroboam also changed the religious calendar and the priesthood. Jeroboam was introducing his own version of the worship of the Lord.

Jeroboam's polluted religious system was the push that started the Northern Kingdom downhill to corruption and captivity. Gross forms of paganism entered easily once true worship of the Lord was abandoned. More than twenty times the Scriptures call Jeroboam the man "who made Israel sin." When the golden calves were set up and accepted by the Northern Kingdom, that kingdom took a notable step downward. The condition of the Northern Kingdom worsened rapidly when many godly people fled the North and went to live in the South in order to avoid the rampant idolatry (cf. 2 Chron. 11:14–17).

A Comparison of the Two Kingdoms

	North	South
Name	Israel	Judah
First King	Jeroboam	Rehoboam
Tribes	10	2
Duration	209 years	345 years
Dynasties	9	1
Kings	20	20
Capital	Samaria	Jerusalem
Conquered by	Assyria	Babylon
Conquered in	721 B.C.	605 B.C.
Last King	Hoshea	Zedekiah

In the Southern Kingdom, however, Rehoboam proved to be an inept and evil king. The glory of Solomon's day faded quickly during Rehoboam's seventeen-year reign (15:21–31). And life was made worse by the war with Jeroboam that continued throughout his reign.

Rulers in the Era of the Monarchy

United Kingdom

King	Years of reign	Date B.C.
Saul	32	1043
David	40	1011
Solomon	40	971

Divided Kingdom

Southern Kings	Years of reign	Date B.C.
Rehoboam	17	931
Abijam	3	913
Asa	41	911
		910
		909
		885
		885
		885
		885
		874
Jehoshaphat	25	870
		853
		852
Jehoram	8	848
Ahaziah	1	841
Athaliah	7	841
Joash	40	835
		814
		798
Amaziah	29	796
		782
Uzziah	52	767
		753
		752
		752
		742
Jotham	16	740
Ahaz	16	732
Hezekiah	29	715
Manasseh	55	687

Northern Kings	Years of reign
Jeroboam I	22
Nadab	2
Baasha	24
Elah	2
Zimri	7 days
Tibni	3
Omri	11
Ahab	22
Ahaziah	2
Jehoram	12
Jehu	28
Jehoahaz	17
Jehoash	16
Jeroboam II	41
Zechariah	6 months
Shallum	1 month
Menahem	10
Pekahiah	2
Pekah	20
Hoshea	10

Single Kingdom

King	Years of reign	Date B.C.
Amon	2	642
Josiah	31	640
Jehoahaz	3 months	609
Jehoiakim	11	609
Jehoiachin	3 months	598
Zedekiah	11	597
Fall of Jerusalem		587

Key:
Good King—basically righteous
Kings who particularly influenced history
Founders of a dynasty

defeated the combined forces of Assyria and Egypt and emerged as the world power. Nebuchadnezzar and his Babylonian army then came down and subjugated Judah. In the course of the next years, Nebuchadnezzar would come a total of three times to Judah.

605 B.C.

Jehoiakim was king of Judah. Judah became a subject nation to Babylon, paying annual taxes. Judah was allowed to have her own king. Some captives and treasure were taken back to Babylon (Dan. 1:2).

597 B.C.

When Jehoiakim refused to pay the tax, Nebuchadnezzar returned. A new king on the throne, Jehoiachin, submitted to him. The king, the rest of the Temple treasure, and some 10,000 captives were taken back to Babylon.

586 B.C.

With Zedekiah on the throne of Judah, once again Judah withheld paying taxes. Nebuchadnezzar returned, destroying the city of Jerusalem and removing the last king of Judah.

With this third coming of Nebuchadnezzar, the Southern Kingdom went into captivity, and the era of the monarchy ended.

12.
1 & 2 Chronicles

INTRODUCTION TO 1 AND 2 CHRONICLES

Authorship and Date of 1 and 2 Chronicles

The author of the Chronicles compiled these books from as many as ten different sources (1 Chron. 9:1; 2 Chron. 12:15). Tradition says that Ezra the scribe wrote these books, and he was certainly qualified to do so (Ezra 7:10–11). It has been suggested by many that the book of Ezra and the Chronicles were actually one consecutive history when they were first written (cf. Ezra 1:1–3 with 2 Chron. 36:22–23). If Ezra was the author, then a date after the captivity of about 450 B.C. is likely.

Purpose of 1 and 2 Chronicles

These books are complementary to 1 and 2 Samuel and 1 and 2 Kings. They were intended to strengthen the remnant of the nation who had made it through the period of the Babylonian Captivity. They needed to be reminded that the Lord was still with them and that they still had a glorious future because God was faithful to His covenants. The nation's apostasy had brought it down, but the nation would rise again.

Relief showing musicians captured by Assyria.

1 and 2 Chronicles

Basic Outline of 1 and 2 Chronicles

1 CHRONICLES

I. The Genealogies (chaps. 1–9)

II. The Reign of King Saul (chap. 10)

III. The Reign of King David (chaps. 11–29)

2 CHRONICLES

I. The United Kingdom Under King Solomon (chaps. 1–9)

II. The Southern Kingdom Under Judean Kings (chaps. 10–36)

This historian's purpose is to show that the true glory of the Hebrew nation was found in its covenant relationship to God, as safeguarded by the prescribed forms of worship in the temple and administered by the divinely ordained priesthood under the protection of the divinely authorized dynasty of David. Always the emphasis is upon that which is sound and valid in Israel's past as furnishing a reliable basis for the task of reconstruction which lay ahead. Great stress is placed upon the rich heritage of Israel and its unbroken connection with the patriarchal beginnings (hence the prominence accorded to genealogical lists).[1]

Chronicles, written after the Babylonian captivity, was both an encouragement and a warning. It was given to encourage Israel with the truth that God was not through with them. It was a warning that future apostasy or idolatry would again be dealt with severely

Special Considerations on 1 and 2 Chronicles

The Relationships of Chronicles
Because the contents of these books is repetitious of material in other neighboring books, it is helpful to see the relationship of Chronicles to other Old Testament materials. This can be quickly seen by consulting the charts opposite.

The Babylonian Captivity
The captivity of Judah officially lasted from 605–536 B.C., a period of seventy years. The prophet Jeremiah had not only warned the people of a coming captivity but also specified the length (Jer. 25:11; 29:10). The reason that the captivity lasted seventy years (and not fifty or one hundred years) is given in 2 Chronicles 36:21. Seventy times the nation had violated God's command to let the land rest every seventh (sabbath) year (cf. Lev.

Relationship

1 Chronicles		2 Chronicles	
1 Samuel	2 Samuel	1 Kings	2 Kings

Comparison

SAMUEL–KINGS

1. Viewed both North and South
2. Emphasis on the Throne
3. Civil/political history
4. Emphasis on the prophet
5. Wars prominent
6. Indictment of the two nations

CHRONICLES

1. Viewed only the South
2. Emphasis on the Temple
3. Sacred history
4. Emphasis on the priest
5. Wars less prominent
6. Encouragement of the remnant

Important Data About 1 and 2 Chronicles

1. Key Word: Temple
2. Key Chapter: 12—David made King of Israel
3. Key Verse: 2 Chron. 7:14
4. Key Characters: David, Solomon, Asa, Jehoshaphat, and Hezekiah
5. Meaning of "Chronicles": Suggests that what is recorded are the official annals of the important affairs in the lives of Israel's kings
6. Geography of Chronicles: The land of Israel

25:1–7; 26:34, 43). Israel was not to plant or harvest during that year. But since the nation would not let the land rest voluntarily, God removed them from the land.

The years of the Babylonian captivity were painful but profitable ones for Judah. The pain of being in captivity to a pagan nation, of seeing Jerusalem burned and sacked, of witnessing the end of the monarchy, and of having no place to sacrifice and worship was terrible. But these years also brought great benefit to the people. They learned that serving idols was foolish, and, for the most part, they were cured of their idolatry. They also developed a new love and loyalty to the Scriptures. They had no temple and no functioning priesthood, but they did have God's Word. It is commonly

The Period of Captivity in Babylon

The period of captivity			
Last Kings in Judah	Zerubbabel	Ezra	Nehemiah

586		458	444
605 · · · · · 70 years · · · · · · · 536		478 Esther becomes queen	

believed that the synagogue, a local gathering place for the reading and teaching of Scripture, originated during the Babylonian captivity.

(a) The Jews in Babylon

Little is known of this period of history, since no "foundational book" covers it. What can be known about the Jews in Babylon is gleaned from Ezekiel, Daniel, and Ezra. The initial years in Babylon were discouraging ones (Ps. 137). Evidently, the Jews generally were not assimilated into Babylonian life but remained separate in detention camps (Ezek. 1:1; 3:15). Some, like Daniel and his three friends, were part of the court of the king. But even these never lost their Jewish identity (Dan. 5:13). Although as the years went by greater assimilation into Babylonian life probably took place, many were ready to "go home" when the opportunity came along.

(b) The Jews Left in Palestine

A great deal of information is available about those days immediately after the destruction of Jerusalem in 586 B.C. The prophet Jeremiah was allowed by Nebuchadnezzar to stay in Palestine. It is Jeremiah who records the situa-

tion of the Jews who remained in the land (Jer. 40–44).

When Jerusalem was destroyed, the town of Mizpah became the political center of Judah and the new provincial capital. A Jew by the name of Gedaliah was selected by Nebuchadnezzar as the first governor of the area. Nebuchadnezzar probably thought it best to allow the Jews to have a Jew ruling over them, as long as he was not a king. With the population now greatly reduced there would be little chance that any large-scale rebellion could take place; thus very few Babylonian soldiers were left behind to aid Gedaliah at Mizpah. The number of people ruled over by Gedaliah was probably less than 50,000.[2] Gedaliah's rule was quite short, perhaps lasting two or three months. He was assassinated in office by Ishmael, who was part of the irreconcilable resistance party, which was based in Ammon. Jeremiah and the inhabitants were taken captive but were rescued by Johanan and a group loyal to Gedaliah. But fearing retaliation by the Babylonians (for the murder of the governor, Gedaliah), the group headed by Johanan retreated to a spot near Bethlehem and pondered their next move. Jeremiah was asked to

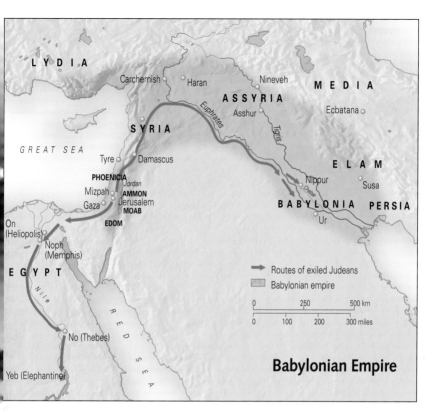

Babylonian Empire

Routes of exiled Judeans
Babylonian empire

inquire of the Lord as to what they should do. Ten days later Jeremiah returned with a word from God. The people were told to stay in the land and not to go down to Egypt, as they were now contemplating. But they would not listen to Jeremiah. Instead they fled to Egypt, forcing Jeremiah to go with them. With the departure of this group, there were almost no Jews left in the land.

SUMMARY OF
1 AND 2 CHRONICLES

1 CHRONICLES

The Genealogies (chaps. 1–9)

These lists trace the lineage of Israel, beginning with Adam and ending with those of the Babylonian captivity. They reveal the hand of God at work during those many years as He selected certain ones to fulfill His purposes.

This genealogy is important in tracing the line of the Messiah. These genealogies are not exhaustive, but are carefully selected. It is plain that the author is most interested in the line of David, the tribe of Levi, and the tribes of Judah and Benjamin.[3]

The Reign of King Saul (chap. 10)

Even though Saul reigned for thirty-two years, little is given about his rule. His unfaithfulness and disobedience receive a brief treatment in order to contrast him with God's choice of a godly king, David.

The Reign of David (chaps. 11–29)

David is the standard used in Scripture for a righteous king. He is seen bringing the nation of Israel together and making it into a powerful force for the Lord. Emphasis is placed on David's desire to make Jerusalem the religious capital of the land and on his desire to build a temple for the Lord.

2 CHRONICLES

The United Kingdom Under King Solomon (chaps. 1–9)

In 2 Chronicles the history of Solomon's reign centers on two visions he received: one at Gibeon (1:1–13) and the other at Jerusalem (7:12–22). Because of his first vision, Solomon is given unusual wisdom from God, thus enabling him to build the Temple and lead Israel in God's paths of righteousness. The second vision took place in the Temple itself. God promised blessing and prosperity for obedience, but discipline for disobedience.

The Southern Kingdom Under Judean Kings (chaps. 10–36)

The emphasis in this section is on the godly kings of Judah who ruled after Solomon in the Southern Kingdom during both the divided and single kingdom periods. The focus is on Asa (14:1–16:14), Jehoshaphat (17:1–20:37), Hezekiah (29:1–32:33), and Josiah (34:1–35:27). Evil kings are given little space by the author. The final chapter describes the fall and deportation of Judah.

13.
Ezra & Esther

EZRA

INTRODUCTION TO EZRA

Authorship and Date of Ezra

Tradition says that Ezra himself wrote this book. It is clear that he was certainly capable of doing so, as he is called "a man of letters" (7:11). With Ezra as the author, the date of writing would be about 450 B.C.

Purpose of Ezra

The purpose of the book of Ezra is to record the faithfulness of God in the reestablishing of the Jews in their land.

Special Considerations on Ezra

Years Covered by Ezra

The entire book of Ezra covers a period of about eighty years. There is a large gap between chapters 6 and 7, where there is no recorded history.

Background Points on Ezra

In order to understand the events surrounding the restoration of the people of Judah to their land, several facts need to be grasped, including the chronology of the period and the Persian kings who ruled during this time.

(a) The Chronology of the Restoration

See chart on the following page.

(b) The People of the Restoration

It was the Southern Kingdom of Judah that was taken captive to Babylon, and it was the Southern Kingdom that returned to the land of Palestine. But it must be kept in mind that

Ezra Basic Outline of Ezra

I. The Return Under Zerubbabel (chaps. 1–6)

II. The Return Under Ezra (chaps. 7–10)

The Chronology of the Restoration

Persian king	Dates	Biblical characters	Scripture	Event
Cyrus	539–530	Zerubbabel Joshua Haggai Zechariah	Ezra 1–4 –	First return Temple begun then stopped
Cambyses	530–521	–	–	No work on Temple
Darius I	521–486	Haggai Zechariah	Ezra 4–6	Temple work completed
Xerxes (Ahasuerus)	486–465	Esther Mordecai	Esther 1–10	Story of Jews' preservation
Artaxerxes	465–423	Ezra Nehemiah Malachi	Ezra 7–10 Nehemiah	Second return under Ezra Third return Nehemiah Ministry of Malachi

END OF OLD TESTAMENT HISTORY

Important Data About Ezra

1. Key Words: Spiritual Restoration
2. Key Chapter: 6—The rebuilding of the Temple
3. Key Verses: 1:1–4; 6:14–15
4. Key Characters: Zerubbabel, Joshua the high priest, and Ezra
5. Meaning of "Ezra": Named after its principal character
6. Geography of Ezra: Babylon and Palestine

there were elements of the northern tribes present also. Sometimes the northern tribes are called the "ten lost tribes." They were not lost in the sense of disappearing. The Northern Kingdom ceased to exist as a separate kingdom, but there were significant numbers from the northern tribes living in the South.

There were several emigrations from the North to the South. At the time of the division of the kingdom many elected to remain under the Davidic king (1 Kings 12:23; 2 Chron. 11:14–16). And again in King Asa's day many came from the North (2 Chron. 15:9). Even after the fall of the Northern Kingdom in 721 B.C., northerners with a heart for the Lord (and still living in the northern area) joined with Hezekiah (2 Chron. 30:11) and later with Josiah (2 Chron. 34:9).

During the captivity, the prophet Ezekiel ministered to the "House of Israel" (3:1–5), which would indicate that even in captivity there was a mingling of the two kingdoms.

At the time of the restoration, the tribes of Judah and Benjamin were definitely the leaders (Ezra 1:5). Yet, the northern cities of Bethel and Ai are included among those in the return (2:28).

Ezra 7:7 records that "there went up some of the children of Israel." At the dedication of the temple, a sin offering was made for all of the twelve tribes (Ezra 6:17). Later another burnt offering was made by those who had come out of the captivity for all the twelve tribes of Israel (Ezra 8:35). These returned exiles certainly seemed to consider themselves as representatives of the whole nation. Furthermore, Zechariah . . . addressed his messages to Judah and Israel (Zech. 1:19; 8:13; 10:6).[1]

It can be said with certainty that all of Israel "came home" in the era of restoration. Certainly in New Testament times all the tribes were in evidence (Luke 2:36; Matt. 10:6; Acts 26:6–7; James 1:1). And all twelve tribes will be part of the final, great restoration of Israel (Ezek. 36:22–32; 37:11–22).

(c) Notable Dates in Ezra

538: The edict of Cyrus, which permitted the Jews to return to their homeland

537: The return of some 50,000 Jews under

The famous Cyrus cylinder, which showed the Persian monarch's policy of assisting nations such as the Jews to return and rebuild their cities and temples.

the leadership of Zerubbabel

536: The altar for sacrificing rebuilt

535: Work on the Temple begun then stopped

535–520: No further work on the Temple

520: Decree of Cyrus confirmed by Darius I; he aids in the construction of the Temple; the prophet Haggai begins his ministry

516: The completion and dedication of the Temple

458: Second return to Judah, led by Ezra

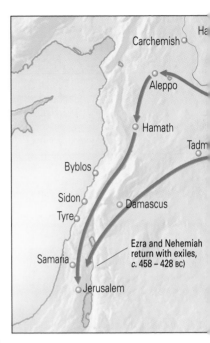

Ezra and Nehemiah return with exiles, c. 458 – 428 BC)

SUMMARY OF EZRA

The Return Under Zerubbabel (Chaps. 1–6)

The Decree of Cyrus (1)
The Persian Empire had defeated and taken over the empire of Babylon in 539 B.C. The Persian government had established itself but still desired the loyalty of its new subjects. Most likely with the help of Daniel, Cyrus issued a decree allowing the Jews to return to their homeland and rebuild their Temple.

The Return to Palestine (2)
Those who were willing to leave Babylon and return to the desolate land of Palestine were carefully listed. Zerubbabel would lead a group of almost 50,000 (2:64–65).

Rebuilding the Temple (3)
Upon arriving in the land, the first order of business was to rebuild the sacrificial altar (3:2). Then preliminary work was done on the Temple, clearing away debris and laying the foundation (3:10).

The Opposition to Rebuilding (4)
Not everyone was glad to see the Jews back in their land. Some made it their business to oppose the Temple project by threatening the Jews and also by hiring lawyers to thwart them in the law courts (4:1–5). The enemies of the Jews succeeded in stopping the work for fifteen years.

The Return to Rebuilding (5)
Challenged and motivated by the prophets Haggai and Zechariah, the people realized the need to get back to Temple building. They came to understand that they had been disobedient and unbelieving. And even though the circumstances had not changed, they were back to work and saw God work on their behalf.

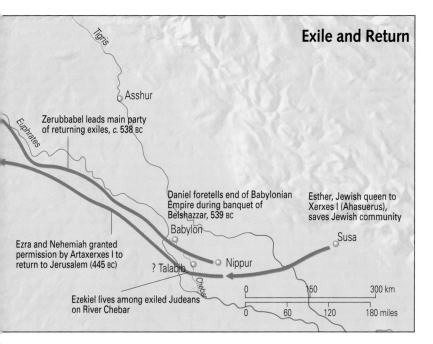

Exile and Return

Zerubbabel leads main party of returning exiles, *c.* 538 BC

Daniel foretells end of Babylonian Empire during banquet of Belshazzar, 539 BC

Esther, Jewish queen to Xerxes I (Ahasuerus), saves Jewish community

Ezra and Nehemiah granted permission by Artaxerxes I to return to Jerusalem (445 BC)

Ezekiel lives among exiled Judeans on River Chebar

Asshur

Tigris

Euphrates

Babylon

? Talabib

Nippur

Chebar

Susa

| 0 | 150 | 300 km |
| 0 | 60 | 120 | 180 miles |

The Temple Completed (6)

After four years of hard work the construction was finished and the Temple was dedicated (6:14–18).

The Return Under Ezra (Chaps. 7–10)

The Decree of Artaxerxes (7)

About eighty years after the first return, under Zerubbabel, Ezra the scribe returned with 1,500 people. Ezra undoubtedly had not been born when the first return took place. His purpose in going to the land was to bring a substantial offering to help the people there and to teach the law of God.

The Return to Palestine (8)

The people of the land were glad for the financial relief brought by Ezra, and Ezra was delighted to finally see Jerusalem.

Reformation Under Ezra (9)

Unfortunately, the people of Israel were once again beginning to compromise God's laws, especially in the matter of marrying pagans. Ezra knew the law, and he knew recent history. He knew that if the situation was not dealt with, more disciplinary action from God would be forthcoming. It was a brokenhearted man who cried to the Lord and mourned greatly (9:1– 3). Many observed Ezra and came to realize the sinfulness of their disobedience. Ezra was the catalyst that made them do the right thing. One godly man, who knows and obeys the Word of God, can impact large numbers of people. Revival (which is a new beginning of obedience) came to the people of the nation of Israel.

ESTHER

This book complements Ezra. It describes a fascinating story of God's providence that transpired back in Persia while many of God's people were resettling Palestine.

INTRODUCTION TO ESTHER

Authorship and Date of Esther

Once again the author is not identified. But it is likely that the author was a Jew who lived

---

Basic Outline of Esther

Esther

I Royal Crisis for God's People (Chaps. 1–5)
- A. Queen Vashti Deposed (1)
- B. Esther Becomes Queen (2)
- C. Haman's Murderous Plot (3)
- D. Mordecai's Intercession (4)
- E. Esther Receives Favor (5)

II. Divine Protection for God's People (Chaps. 6–10)
- A. Mordecai Receives Honor (6)
- B. Haman's Execution (7)
- C. The Jews Avenged (8)
- D. Purim Instituted (9)
- E. Mordecai Becomes Premier (10)

Important Data About Esther

1. Key Word: Providence of God
2. Key Chapter: 6—The hand of God changes the situation
3. Key Verses: 4:13–14; 6:13; 8:17; 9:26–28
4. Key Characters: Mordecai, Esther, Haman, and Ahasuerus
5. Meaning of "Esther": The book is named after the key character in the story
6. Geography of Esther: The land of Persia

---

through the events described in this book. His knowledge of Persian words and customs and his detailed descriptions of the palace of Susa (1:6–8; 7:8) strongly suggest one who was an eyewitness. Based on Esther 9:20, many believe that Mordecai the Jew penned this book. Others do not think that the words of praise in chapter 10 would have been written by Mordecai of himself. But if the book was written during the days of Ahasuerus (Xerxes) then the date would be about 475 B.C.

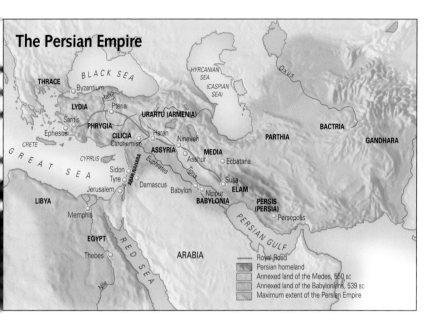

The Persian Empire

Royal Road
Persian homeland
Annexed land of the Medes, 550 BC
Annexed land of the Babylonians, 539 BC
Maximum extent of the Persian Empire

Purpose of Esther

The book was written to show God's providential care for His people even while they were in captivity and in a poor spiritual condition. Because of the Abrahamic Covenant, God would never allow these descendants of Abraham to be exterminated. He still blesses those who bless Israel and, as in this case, curses those who curse Israel.

Special Considerations on Esther

Esther's story took place in the time period of the book of Ezra. These events occurred between the first and second returns, and

therefore come between Ezra 6 and 7. (See the chart "The Chronology of the Restoration," page 146.)

SUMMARY OF ESTHER

Royal Crisis for God's People (chaps. 1–5)

Queen Vashti Deposed (1)

The first chapter sets the stage for the story by informing the reader of the removal of the Persian queen Vashti. Her husband, King Ahasuerus, demanded that she appear before him and the leaders of the nation. Perhaps in a state of drunkenness (1:10), the king was actu-

Jewish people celebrate Esther's victory over the wicked Haman at the festival of Purim. They make a great noise, often using wooden rattles, whenever Haman's name is mentioned.

ally demanding a lewd display on the part of the queen. At any rate, she refused. In his anger and humiliation, the king removed her from her position as queen (1:12, 19).

Esther Becomes Queen (2)

In order to fill the vacancy of queen, a nation-wide beauty contest was held (2:3). Young women would join the king's harem, and then the king would decide which would be queen. Esther the Jewess became part of this situation (2:5–8). Esther had lost her parents and was raised by Mordecai, her cousin. He instructed her not to reveal that she was Jewish. (These two do not seem to be sterling examples of spirituality, as were Daniel and Joseph.) Esther was winner of the contest, and she became the queen.

Haman's Murderous Plot (3)

The king elevated Haman to a position of great authority in the kingdom of Persia. But Haman became offended by the Jew Mordecai. In his anger, Haman decided to get rid of all the Jews.

Mordecai's Intercession (4)

When Mordecai came to understand that the

Jews were scheduled for destruction because of his actions, he persuaded Esther the queen to intervene on behalf of the Jews.

Esther Receives Favor (5)

At the risk of her own life, Esther approached the king. She asked him to come to a banquet, and it was at the banquet that she would make her appeal. Haman was to come also.

Divine Protection for God's People (chaps. 4–10)

Mordecai Receives Honor (6)

Through a set of divinely arranged circumstances Haman was forced to publicly praise Mordecai the Jew, the man he hated. To Haman's wife and friends this indicated that Haman was doomed (6:13). Their viewpoint suggests that the unseen hand of God had often moved on behalf of His people.

Haman's Execution (7)

At the banquet Esther pleaded for her own life and pointed to Haman as the villain in the matter. The king, who did not have the slightest idea of what was going on, was enraged and ordered the execution of Haman.

The Jews Avenged (8)

The law that allowed the Jews to be killed could not be changed. In Persian society the law was greater than any person, even the king. And once a law had been set in place it could not be annulled. But another law could be instituted that could counteract the previous law. This was done, and the Jews were allowed to defend themselves with no penalty for doing so.

Purim Instituted (9)

The annual Jewish feast of Purim came out of these events in Persia and celebrates the Jews' deliverance from their enemies.

Mordecai Becomes Premier (10)

The king elevated Mordecai to a position of great prominence in his kingdom. In that position, Mordecai was used to help the Jews of the Persian Empire.

14.

Nehemiah

INTRODUCTION TO NEHEMIAH

Authorship and Date of Nehemiah

Nehemiah himself was probably the author of this book (1:1). The date of writing would be about 425 B.C., in the reign of Artaxerxes, king of Persia. (See chart "The Chronology of the Restoration," page 146.)

Purpose of Nehemiah

The book was written to show the work of God through a godly leader, Nehemiah. The book records the building, fortifying, and reestablishing of the city of Jerusalem. The book also reveals the beautiful balance in the life of Nehemiah between zealous human effort and planning, and divine empowering.

Special Considerations on Nehemiah

Years Covered by Nehemiah
The book of Nehemiah covers a period of twelve years from 444–432 B.C. This is based on the two time notations in 1:1 and 13:6, the twentieth and the thirty-second years of Artaxerxes' reign.

Background Points on Nehemiah

(a) The Historical Setting
When Nehemiah, living in Persia in 445 B.C., received news that Jerusalem's walls were broken down and its gates were burned, his

---

Important Data About Nehemiah

1. Key Words: Political restoration
2. Key Chapter: 6—The rebuilding of Jerusalem's walls
3. Key Verses: 1:4–11; 2:17; 5:14; 6:15
4. Key Characters: Nehemiah, Artaxerxes, and Ezra
5. Meaning of "Nehemiah": Named after the central person in the narrative
6. Geography of Nehemiah: Persia and Palestine

response was that of intense sorrow (1:3–4). It is highly unlikely that Nehemiah's sudden grief was due to Nebuchadnezzar's destruction of Jerusalem over a century earlier (in 586 B.C.). Ezra 4:6–23, which provides some background information for the book of Nehemiah, furnishes a plausible answer. This passage records the opposition of the Jews' enemies in Palestine from the days of Cyrus to the days of Artaxerxes (4:5, 7). In the days of Artaxerxes, some Jews were evidently beginning to rebuild the walls of Jerusalem (4:12). This probably refers to some kind of activity connected with

Artist's impression of the rebuilding of the walls of the Jewish capital city, Jerusalem.

the coming of Ezra in 458 B.C. When informed of the building and of the Jews' past rebellion, King Artaxerxes ordered a halt to the building (4:21). He did not order the walls and gates destroyed, but the enemies of Israel took it upon themselves to do so. Hearing about this terrible setback, a frustrated and depressed Nehemiah agonized over Israel's future.

(b) The Contemporaries of Nehemiah
When Nehemiah arrived at Jerusalem in 444 B.C., Ezra the scribe-priest had been there for more than a decade. The Scriptures are clear that these two men of God ministered and worked together (Neh. 8:1–18; 12:26). After staying in Jerusalem for twelve years, Nehemiah returned to Persia in 432 B.C. (the thirty-second year of Artaxerxes, 13:6). After an undetermined length of time, he returned to Jerusalem (13:6). He found that certain sins (such as withholding the tithe, intermarriage with pagans, etc.) were quite visible among the people. The prophet Malachi dealt with the same sins, which strongly suggests that either Malachi ministered while Nehemiah was in Jerusalem the second time, or he prophesied during those days when Nehemiah was absent from Jerusalem.

SUMMARY OF NEHEMIAH

Rebuilding the Walls (chaps. 1–7)

Nehemiah's Prayer for the Remnant at Jerusalem (1:1–11)
When informed by his brother Hanani of the desolation of Jerusalem, Nehemiah spent about four months in prayer. He confessed the sin of Israel and prayed for the favor of King Artaxerxes. At this time, Nehemiah was the cupbearer to the king. The position of cupbearer was important in the kingdom of Persia. Nehemiah would have been a man highly trusted by the king.

Nehemiah's Request and Return to Jerusalem (2:1–16)
Since no one was to appear sad or depressed before the king, Nehemiah was afraid when the king noted his sadness (2:1–2). But it provided the opportunity for Nehemiah to request a leave of absence from the king's service in order to go to Jerusalem and rebuild the walls. Nehemiah was given permission to go to Jerusalem, and he was given access to building materials for the project. Upon arriving in Jerusalem, Nehemiah quietly surveyed the damage and then presented his plan to the people.

Nehemiah's Exhortations to Rebuild the Walls (2:17–3:32)
Nehemiah identifed himself with the people and the problem as he addressed them and shared his vision (2:17–18). The project was well organized and involved everyone.

Nehemiah's Response to Opposition (4:1–6:19)
Even when a person is doing the will of God, there can be problems and stiff opposition. Nehemiah faced a series of people and situations that could have brought the rebuilding project to a halt (4:1–4, 11; 5:1; 6:1). Opposition came from the enemies on the outside and from the Jews themselves on the inside.

The Gates, Walls, and Towers of Jerusalem

Tower of Hananel

Fish Gate

Sheep Gate

Inspection Gate

Old Gate

Original Zion

Extended by
the kings

Temple

East gate

Horse Gate

Lower City

Furnace Tower

Great
Projecting
Tower

Wall of Ophel

Kidron Gate

Valley Gate

Gihon Spring

Water Gate

Projecting
Tower

Cheesemakers Valley

City of David

Hinnom Valley

Hezekiah's Tunnel

Pool of
Shelah

Fountain Gate

KIDRON VALLEY

Refuse Gate

Probable city wall under
Nehemiah

0   100   200 Meters

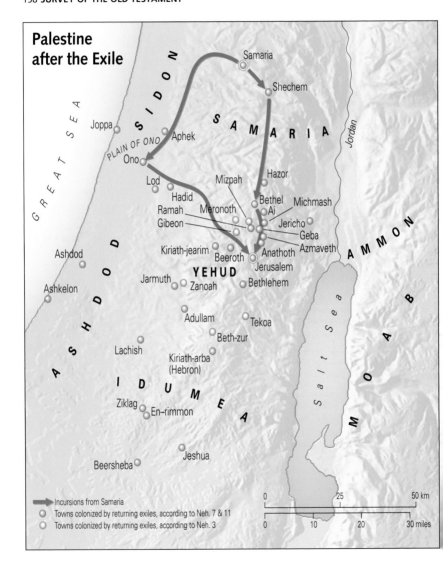

Palestine after the Exile

GREAT SEA

SIDON

Joppa

PLAIN OF ONO

Aphek

Ono

Lod

Hadid

Ramah

Gibeon

Kiriath-jearim

SAMARIA

Samaria

Shechem

Jordan

Hazor

Mizpah

Meronoth

Bethel

Ai

Michmash

Jericho

Geba

Azmaveth

Anathoth

Beeroth

Jerusalem

YEHUD

Ashdod

Ashkelon

ASHDOD

Jarmuth

Zanoah

Bethlehem

Adullam

Tekoa

Beth-zur

Lachish

Kiriath-arba

(Hebron)

IDUMEA

Ziklag

En–rimmon

Jeshua

Beersheba

AMMON

Salt Sea

MOAB

Incursions from Samaria

Towns colonized by returning exiles, according to Neh. 7 & 11

Towns colonized by returning exiles, according to Neh. 3

0		25		50 km

0	10	20	30 miles

But Nehemiah, a man of prayer and wisdom, brought the people through the difficult times. In just fifty-two days of work, the walls of Jerusalem were finished (6:15).

Nehemiah's Registration of the People (7:1–73)

Once the walls were completed, thus affording some protection, Nehemiah asked one-tenth of the people to come and live within the city. He also organized a militia to defend the city. It should be noted that although the walls were essentially finished, much more work needed to be done both in strengthening the walls and rebuilding the city itself.

Revival and Reform (chaps. 8–13)

The Great Bible Reading Led by Ezra (8:1–18)

It is a mistake to think that Nehemiah was concerned only about the physical restoration of the nation. Nehemiah was deeply committed to teaching the nation to live according to its "constitution" (the Mosaic law code). Ezra read from the law and explained its meaning to the thousands who gathered (8:1–8).

Revival and Its Results (9:1–10:39)

Any genuine revival is based squarely on the Word of God. (Revival is a new beginning of obedience to God and His Word.) Any genuine revival will bring about changed behavior. These chapters record not only the confession of sin (9:2–3) but also a change in living (10:30–39).

The People in the Land (11:1–12:26)

It was necessary to populate the city of Jerusalem, once the walls were completed (11:1). Nehemiah was concerned that the city be repopulated by those of pure Jewish descent. Nehemiah handled this and other issues of organization in a forthright manner.

Reform and Results (13:1–31)

When Nehemiah left Jerusalem, much of his influence left also. During his absence, certain sins were once again tolerated in national life. But when Nehemiah returned, he zealously dealt with the offenders (13:7–11, 23–25). Nehemiah knew that to tolerate clear violations of the law would inevitably bring discipline from God.

With the reforms of Nehemiah the Old Testament closes. There is no inspired record for the next four hundred years of Israel's history. The silence of God was finally broken when the angel Gabriel appeared in the holy place of the Temple announcing the coming birth of John the Baptist, the one who would prepare the way for Jesus the Messiah (Luke 1:11–18).

PART 3

The Poetic Books

15.
Hebrew
Poetry

INTRODUCTION TO HEBREW POETRY

Poetry is found everywhere in the Old Testament Scriptures, but six entire books of poetry were written during the era of the monarchy. The time of the united monarchy would be considered Israel's "golden age of literature." These days of peace, in the reigns of David and Solomon (found in the foundational books of 2 Samuel and 1 Kings), were the most productive in the writing of the songs and poems that became such an important part of life in Israel. These books of poetry spoke not only to ancient Israel but have had a continuing impact on God's people.

Reflected in this literature are the problems, experiences, beliefs, philosophies, and attitudes of the Israelites. Such a wide variety of interests are expressed that these writings well-nigh have a universal appeal. The frequent use by the common people throughout the world and the voluminous literature written since Old Testament times indicate that the poetical books deal with problems and truths familiar to all mankind.[1]

THE BOOKS OF HEBREW POETRY

The poetical books do indeed speak to the issues and needs experienced by believers then and now. (1) *Job* wrestles with the problem of suffering that righteous people endure in this life. (2) The *Psalms* basically are songs of praise, though they express the full range of human emotions. (3) The book of *Proverbs* provides valuable insights into all realms of life and gives needed instruction on living wisely. (4) *Ecclesiastes* approaches the matter of wise living from a unique point of view, but makes clear that apart from a right relationship with God life is empty. (5) *Song of Solomon* is a

Relief depicting Jews in exile in Babylon mourning beside the river.

dramatic poem that expresses the joys and dangers of human love. (6) *Lamentations* is an expression of deep human grief coupled with trust in a covenant-keeping God.

TYPES OF HEBREW POETRY

There are different ways of categorizing Hebrew poetry, but the following five types are the main kinds.[2] (1) *Lyric* poems are so named because they were originally designed to be accompanied by music. Most of the psalms fall into this category. (2) *Didactic* poetry intended to teach people to observe and evaluate life. The mind, rather than the emotions, was appealed to. Proverbs and Ecclesiastes would be considered didactic. (3) *Prophetic* poems are not found in these six books of poetry, but rather in Isaiah and some other places. (4) *Elegiac* poetry records human grief and sorrow. The Lamentations of Jeremiah fit into this category. (5) *Dramatic* poems, such as Job and the Song of Solomon, convey ideas and truth through dialogue and monologue, much like modern plays.

PARALLELISM IN HEBREW POETRY

Unlike poems and verse that we are most familiar with, Hebrew poetry is not achieved by rhyme. The basic structure of Hebrew poetry is parallelism.

We do not find any emphasis at all on rhyme and very little on metre compared to that of other languages. The principal feature is that of parallelism, the idea that the second or following lines of a strophe somehow parallel the thought of the first.[3]

In the structure of Hebrew poetry, a statement is made in the first line and then the second line repeats or expands or contrasts that thought. It is the "thought" or "sense" rhyme in Hebrew poetry that makes it much easier to translate these great truths from Hebrew into other languages.

Numerous kinds of parallelism could be mentioned. Five will be defined here, though the first three are usually considered to be the main types:[4] (1) *synonymous:* the second line repeats the same thought as the first line in very similar or identical terms (e.g., Pss. 24:1; 19:2); (2) *antithetic:* the second line contrasts the idea of the first line (e.g., Pss. 1:6; 37:9);

(3) *synthetic:* the second (and perhaps later) line(s) completes or enlarges upon the thought of the first line (e.g., Pss. 2:6; 19:7); (4) *climactic:* a word is built upon until a climax in thought is reached (e.g., Pss. 29:1; 103:1); (5) *emblematic:* a metaphor or simile in one line is used to illustrate the truth of another line (eg., Pss. 42:1; Prov. 25:25).

Hebrew poetry possesses many other features such as beautiful word pictures and figures of speech, acrostic arrangement, similes, metaphors, and personification of ideas or objects. But the value of this portion of the Old Testament is not necessarily found in the variety of literary devices, but in the beautiful balance that exists between the inspiring work of the Holy Spirit and the deepest and widest of human emotion and expression. The believer can not only identify with these writers but is also assured that the truth received is an authoritative, unchanging message from God.

16. Job

INTRODUCTION TO JOB

Authorship and Date of Job

Since the author is not identified in the book, it is not possible to determine authorship and the date of composition. Many men, including Moses and Job himself, have been suggested as authors.[1] Generally speaking, conservative scholars believe that the book was written in the days of King Solomon, though the man Job lived in

Job sat for days with his comforters, trying to understand God's providence.

patriarchal times.[2]

Job was a historical character (cf. Ezek. 14:14, 20; James 5:11). Several facts indicate that he lived in those days after the Flood of Noah and before the time of Moses. First, the length of Job's life points to that time shortly after the Flood in which men had long life spans. Job lived 140 years *after* he had fathered ten children who were adults in the drama and after he had experienced the traumatic events of this story (42:16). Second, Job is seen functioning as a priest for his family, a typical role in the patriarchal days (1:5). And third, the Mosaic law and the important revelations of the prophets are never referred to in all the theological discussions of Job and his friends. It is highly unlikely that they would speak of God and His ways and never refer to the authoritative Scriptures, if they existed at that time. The setting of the book of Job is, therefore, in the days of the patriarchs. The writing of the book, however, may have been much later.

Purpose of Job

The book of Job addresses the issue of the suffering of people who are righteous. Whereas the suffering and distress of the wicked has not been as great a problem to most people, the suffering of people who love and serve the Lord God is another matter. If God is sovereign and loving, then why does He permit His own to experience terrible (and apparently needless) suffering? Although the book of Job might suggest some answers to this issue, an intellectual solution is not really given. A spiritual solution is given; namely, the absolute sover-

Job

Basic Outline of Job

I. The Prologue
(1:1–2:13)

II. Human Wisdom and Suffering
(3:1–37:24)

III. Divine Wisdom and Suffering
(38:1–42:6)

IV. The Epilogue
(42:7–17)

eignty of God. When Job met God, he did not demand answers but humbly submitted himself to his sovereign God, recognizing in a fresh way the Creator-creature relationship.

Important Data About Job

1. Key Word: Suffering, sovereignty
2. Key Chapter: 1—Setting the stage for the drama of Job
3. Key Verses: 1:20–22; 8:3–7; 40:1–2
4. Key Characters: Job, Eliphaz, Bildad, Zophar, and Elihu
5. Meaning of "Job": Named after the main character in the story
6. Geography of Job: Palestine

An Eastern shepherd guards his flock. Psalm 23 is probably the best-known and loved of the Psalms.

Interpretation of some psalms is greatly aided by certain titles and terms that were placed by the authors at the beginning of those psalms. Sometimes there is an explanatory note at the beginning of the psalm that reveals the historical setting of the psalm (e.g., Pss. 7, 34, 51, 54, 56, 57, 59, 60). Sometimes a notation indicates the occasion on which the psalm was to be used (e.g., Pss. 92, 100, 120) or why the psalm was written (e.g., Pss. 81, 84, 85). Other times a musical notation is given that suggests the tune to be used or the way it was to be sung (e.g., Pss. 6, 7, 9). All of these explanatory notes help give a better feel for the psalm.

Again it must be remembered that most of the Psalms were written before the revelations of the prophets, and all of them were written before the New Testament. Therefore, in interpreting the Psalms care must be taken not to incorrectly read later revelation into the statements made by the psalmists.

SUMMARY OF PSALMS

There are numerous types of psalms, and scholars will construct differing lists and categories. It is best not to attempt to come up with a rigid list. The categories given below should not be seen as fixed categories, since often a single psalm will have elements of several psalm types in it. But the following will give a basic idea of the differences that exist in the Psalms.

Jerusalem from the Mount of Olives. Some Psalms were sung as pilgrims descended into the city.

Messianic Psalms

These are psalms that prophetically speak of the Person and the work of the Messiah. Some of these psalms refer only to the Lord Jesus Christ. Others refer to the king on the throne at the time the psalm was composed, but await the final fulfillment in the Lord Jesus Christ (e.g., Pss. 2, 8, 22, 69, 110).

Lament Psalms

In these psalms there is a cry to God for help because of some trouble that the psalmist finds himself (or his nation) in. God is petitioned to act on behalf of the psalmist (or Israel). Within this type of psalm there will be found a confession of trust in God (e.g., Pss. 7, 26, 60).

Testimonial Psalms

The essential feature of this psalm is the declaration by the writer that he will tell others what God has done for him ("I will praise . . ."). The psalm looks back to some moment of need in his life and records how God met that need. It is a testimony (e.g., Pss. 30, 34).

Pilgrim Psalms

Also known as "songs of ascent," these psalms have to do with pilgrimages to the holy city of Jerusalem. These songs were evidently sung as the Israelites ascended to Jerusalem for the great annual feasts (e.g., Pss. 120–134).

Imprecatory Psalms

These are psalms that ask for judgment on

wicked men who are enemies of the writer. These wicked men have not just offended the author but also God who is holy (e.g., Pss. 58, 109).

Penitential Psalms

Mostly written by David, these psalms reveal the heart of the penitent individual, sorrowing over his sin (e.g., Pss. 32, 51).

Wisdom Psalms

These psalms give guidelines to godly people living in this ungodly world. A philosophy of life is offered to the righteous man to help him view life more from God's perspective (e.g., Pss. 37, 73).

Historical Psalms

In the historical psalms, the writer looks back on God's dealings with the nation of Israel. The power and faithfulness of God are spoken of. These psalms often provide a "divine commentary" on some past event in Israel's history, giving added insight to that event (e.g., Pss. 78, 105, 106).

Nature Psalms

The handiwork of God in His creative work is the emphasis of these psalms. The greatness, goodness, and power of God inspired the psalmist to write (e.g., Pss. 8, 19).

The various types of psalms reflect the common experiences of God's people. They help us express ourselves to the Lord in times of great joy, sorrow, frustration, or fear. There is probably no situation of life that some psalm does not directly address.

18. Proverbs

INTRODUCTION TO PROVERBS

Authorship and Date of Proverbs

It is generally agreed that King Solomon wrote a major share of the book of Proverbs. The book itself testifies to his authorship (1:1; 10:1; 25:1), and 1 Kings 4:29–32 records both the great wisdom and the prolific writing of Solomon. Since most of the proverbs were written by Solomon (chaps. 1–29), a date of about 950 B.C. is given for the book.

The final two chapters of the book were written by Agur and King Lemuel. We know nothing of certainty about either of these two men.

Purpose of Proverbs

Proverbs gives wisdom on all areas of human experience. Wisdom is not simply a matter of the intellect—it is viewing life and self from God's perspective, which is the only true and valid perspective. A wise person is able to deal with life's issues and problems with the advantage of God's viewpoint.

A proverb is a brief saying that is used to communicate much truth. In a concise, striking way, truth is expressed so as to be caught by the mind and retained by the memory. The root of the word *proverb* carries the idea of "to govern" or "rule." Therefore, proverbs are wise, concise sayings that are to be used in governing our lives.

Important Data About Proverbs

1. Key Word: Wisdom
2. Key Chapter: 1 and 2—The importance and attaining of wisdom
3. Key Verses: 1:2–7; 1:20–2:7
4. Key Characters: Solomon
5. Meaning of "Proverbs": Refers to short sayings that are designed to govern life and conduct
6. Geography of Proverbs: Israel

Proverbs

Special Considerations on Proverbs

Since Proverbs is a book of poetry, parallelism is the key interpretive element. Synonymous parallelism is often identified in Proverbs by the use of "than," "so," or "as"; antithetic parallelism is recognized by the word "but"; and synthetic parallelism is often identified by the word "and."

The words "wise" and "wisdom" are repeated

All wisdom comes from the Lord, but we have a responsibility to search and seek after wisdom.

many times, along with "knowledge" and "understanding." The key phrase "the fear of the Lord" is found more than a dozen times in the book.

SUMMARY OF PROVERBS

The book of Proverbs was written to bring us to wisdom and into a disciplined life (1:2–7). Solomon is convinced that wisdom begins with a right relationship with God (1:7; 9:10). Until a man "fears the Lord" (meaning he has the proper view of God, which results in a right relationship with God), he has no real hope of living an abundant kind of life. Until a man sees God rightly, he cannot rightly view life (cf.

1 Cor. 1:18–31).

Wisdom continues as the theme in chapters 1 through 9, and it is personified in several places as a woman (1:20–33; 8:1–9:18). She is seen walking in the streets of the city inviting people to come and to receive true understanding from her.

A person's response to wisdom places him into one of four groups: *The wise* is one who heeds and receives the truth and thus becomes discerning; *the naive* is one who does not listen to wisdom and is easily deceived in life, believing what he wants to believe; *the scoffer* is cynical and sarcastic in regard to the wisdom of God and spiritual things, making it impossible to live correctly; *the fool* has rejected God's

We need to study and to learn God's truth and increase in wisdom.

Wisdom is a theme of chapters 1 through 9, and is personified in several places as a woman.

wisdom and as a result is dull and wicked both morally and spiritually. The effect on one's life of either receiving or rejecting wisdom is great (1:24–33).

All wisdom comes from the Lord, but man has a responsibility to search and seek after wisdom (2:1–12). So although the "fear of the Lord" is the beginning of wisdom, man needs to study and to learn God's truth and increase in wisdom (cf. 2 Tim. 2:15). Having true wisdom will keep one from making some terrible errors in judgment (e.g., 7:6–23) and will bring a person into an abundant kind of life (8:35).

After the section on the value of wisdom (1:1–9:18), Proverbs becomes a collection of individual proverbs dealing with a wide range of subjects. In chapters 10–29 there is a general theme of righteous living but no particular order or grouping of these proverbs. Some of the major subjects dealt with in this section are the use and abuse of the tongue, the benefits and blessings of work and diligence, good friends, child training, the positive and negative aspects of sex, wealth, God's guidance, and the blessings of being wise.

Because Proverbs touches on every area of life, it is a favorite book of believers. It is not only relevant to life but shows that God is interested in every area of life.

19. Ecclesiastes

INTRODUCTION TO ECCLESIASTES

Authorship and Date of Ecclesiastes

The authorship of Ecclesiastes is greatly debated. Many hold to Solomonic authorship, whereas others adamantly oppose that position. Some statements in the book make Solomonic authorship difficult. Nevertheless, the best position is still that King Solomon wrote this book. The author does say that he was the "son of David, king in Jerusalem" (1:1, 12). Solomon certainly fits that statement. Furthermore, the wisdom, wealth, and great building projects spoken of in Ecclesiastes (1:13–16; 2:4–10) are obviously true of the life of Solomon (1 Kings 3:12; 4:29– 32; 10:14–29). And Solomon certainly had the time and the money to do all the things discussed in Ecclesiastes.[1]

Seven times the author identifies himself as "Koheleth," or the "Preacher." In many ways Ecclesiastes is a sermon in which "Koheleth" sets forth certain conclusions based on his observations and on certain Old Testament passages.

It is probably best to assume that Solomon wrote this book toward the end of his life, after he had experienced so very much. Solomon had begun his reign walking with the Lord and ruling with great wisdom. But Solomon sinned by turning from the Lord to serve idols, and so experienced life apart from the true God. After he repented and turned back to the Lord, Solomon could reflect insightfully on his failure and his foolishness. He understood experientially the emptiness of living away from the Lord. Since Solomon died in 931 B.C., a date shortly before that would be assigned to this book.

Purpose of Ecclesiastes

Ecclesiastes records man's struggle to find meaning and fulfillment in life. The basic theme is that life is empty and meaningless apart from a right relationship with God. Unless a man comes to know the Creator, nothing in the creation can bring him peace and satisfaction. Everything will be "vain"

A Jewish bride in traditional costume, with its elaborate and colorful headdress.

that genuine love in the context of marital commitment is beautiful, uplifting, and satisfy-ing. It carries with it pleasant memories with-out any guilt or self-reproach.

21. *Lamentations*

INTRODUCTION TO LAMENTATIONS

Authorship and Date of Lamentations

The evidence points to the prophet Jeremiah as the author of Lamentations.

Such evidence includes the following: (1) the Septuagint and Vulgate introductions to the book, which read in part: "Jeremiah sat weeping and lamented with the lamentation over Jerusalem, and said . . . ," (2) Hebrew and Gentile tradition, (3) similarities between Lamentations and poetical portions of Jeremiah . . . , (4) the writer was an eyewitness of Jerusalem's destruction, with a sensitivity of soul (cf. Jer. 9:1; 14:17–22) and an ability to write.[1]

In light of the sequence of events found in 2 Kings 25 and Jeremiah 40–44, it is likely that Jeremiah penned the book at Mizpah in 586 B.C.[2] He was at Mizpah when Jerusalem was burned and reduced to rubble. The deep sorrow expressed in Lamentations suggests a time of

Lamentations

Basic Outline of Lamentations

I. The First Lamentation: Jerusalem's Grief (chap. 1)

II. The Second Lamentation: God's Wrath (chap. 2)

III. The Third Lamentation: Continuing Hope (chap. 3)

IV. The Fourth Lamentation: Sin's Consequences (chap. 4)

V. The Fifth Lamentation: Prayerful Confession (chap. 5)

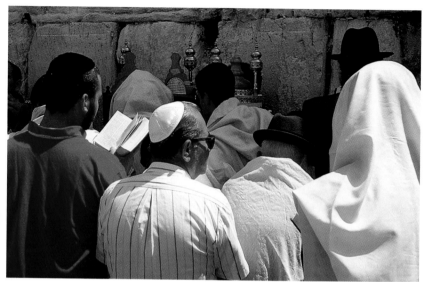

Orthodox Jews praying at Jerusalem's Western Wall often use the words of Lamentations.

writing shortly after the destruction of Jerusalem.

Purpose of Lamentations

The book is a lament over the destruction of Jerusalem at the hands of the Babylonian armies, following months of a devastating siege of the city. It displays enormous emotional and physical pain. This poem is a sequel to the book of Jeremiah.

Special Considerations on Lamentations

The unique feature about the poetry of Lamentations is its acrostic arrangement.

Important Data About Lamentations

1. Key Word: Lament
2. Key Chapter: 3—Hope in the midst of affliction
3. Key Verses: 1:1–12; 3:22–23
4. Key Characters: Jeremiah and Jerusalem (personified)
5. Meaning of "Lamentations": Reflects the dirgelike quality of the poem
6. Geography of Lamentations: Jerusalem

In arrangement the first four chapters are alphabetic acrostics. Each chapter has 22 verses or a multiple thereof. The 22 letters of the Hebrew alphabet are used successfully to begin each verse in 1 and 2. Chapters 3 and 4 allot three and two verses respectively to each Hebrew letter. Although 5 has 22 verses it does not represent an alphabetic acrostic.[3]

It may well be that Jeremiah employed this literary device as a memory aid for his countrymen, who would read this poem.

SUMMARY OF LAMENTATIONS

Lamentations expresses the reaction of one who was an eyewitness and deeply involved in a terrible event. Even though Jeremiah had warned Judah for some forty years that such judgment would come, the event itself was overwhelming.

Great grief is expressed over the wrath of God poured out on Judah (e.g., 3:49). As the covenant people witnessed the removal of their king, the burning of their Temple, and the destruction of their land, they could find no comfort anywhere (e.g., 1:2, 12; 2:7). False prophets were partly to blame for their condition (2:14). The people had not listened to men like Jeremiah, and the nightmare of the long siege came upon them. Starvation and cannibalism became part of life in the city (2:11–12; 4:5–10). In all of this, Jeremiah acknowledged that God was holy, righteous, and faithful (3:21–33). And as the poem ended, he pleaded for mercy, confessing the sin of his people (5:1–22).

PART 4

The Prophetic Books

22. God's Prophetic Messengers

For a thousand years of Israel's history there appeared men (and a few women) who received messages from God and delivered those messages to Israel. These prophets had a profound impact on the national life of Israel. Although they did not appear in unbroken order (cf. 1 Sam. 3:1), they did come on the scene in every era of Israel's history.

THE OFFICE OF THE PROPHETS

The prophet Amos makes clear that prophets were a gift from God (Amos 2:11). The divine origin of the prophetic office is affirmed by Jeremiah, who also reveals that it began with Moses (Jer. 7:25). (Note that God spoke directly to men like Abraham, before Moses, but the prophetic office with its various functions began with Moses.)

A primary passage in understanding the prophetic office is Deuteronomy 18:9–22. In this passage, Moses declared that God would raise up the prophetic institution and that someday a great Prophet would arise. This message was given as Israel prepared to enter the land of Canaan. The first thing Moses told the Israelites was that when they entered the land they were not to involve themselves in the Canaanite practices of witchcraft, spells, omens, spiritism, or similar observances. These wicked, superstitious rituals were not to be used to obtain direction or information. Instead, God would raise up a prophet (Deut. 18:18). At first, Moses seemed to be speaking about just one prophet. But the context of Deuteronomy, as well as the continuing need for the prophetic office over the years does not permit us to understand that only one person is in view.[1] Jesus Christ, of course, would be the great Prophet who would give final and complete fulfillment to this passage.

THE NAMES FOR THE PROPHETS

The Prophet

The primary term for the prophet in the Old Testament is *nabhi*. The origin of this Hebrew word is uncertain even though numerous ideas for the root of the word have been sug-

THE PROPHETIC BOOKS

GROUP ONE

Prophecies during the Divided Kingdom

Prophet	Date	Message to	Rulers
Obadiah	845	Edom	Joram, Jehoram
Joel	830	Judah	Joash
Jonah	780	Nineveh	Jeroboam II
Amos	760	Israel	Jeroboam II
Hosea	750	Israel	Jeroabam II–Hoshea
Isaiah	740	Judah	Uzziah–Hezekiah
Micah	735	Judah	Jotham–Hezekiah

23.

Obadiah

INTRODUCTION TO OBADIAH

Authorship and Date of Obadiah

This shortest of all Old Testament books was written by an unknown prophet named Obadiah (the name means "servant of the Lord"). The author gives no other information about himself, his background, or the time in which he lived. His name is a common one in the Old Testament; about a dozen individuals are so named. All attempts to identify this author with one of the dozen Obadiahs found in the text of the Old Testament have failed.

A date of 845 B.C. is given for this book, making it the earliest of all the prophets. The key to establishing the date of Obadiah is found in verses 10–14 of the book. These verses reveal that an attack was made on the city of Jerusalem, an attack in which the Edomites participated or at least encouraged the attackers. The Old Testament records seven times when Jerusalem was attacked. The second of these attacks (2 Kings 8:20–22; 2 Chron. 21:8– 17) in the days of King Jehoram best fits the event described in Obadiah. At that time, the Philistines and the Arabians attacked Jerusalem. Instead of helping "brother Jacob," the Edomites assisted the enemies of Judah.[1] This event took place about 845 B.C.

Obadiah

Basic Outline of Obadiah

I. The Overthrow of Edom (vv. 1–9)

II. The Offenses of Edom (vv. 10–14)

III. The Outlook for Edom (vv. 15–21)

Amos

Because of the temporary balance of power in the world, they had been relatively free of war and had therefore enjoyed a peaceful situation. The nation had become brazen in its idolatry and moral corruption, as calf worship and Canaanite idolatry were firmly established in the Northern Kingdom. Material prosperity only made matters worse. The people were characterized by wealth, moral laxity, and

The site of the corrupt city of Bethel.

religious indifference. It was the task of Amos (and later Hosea) to try to stop wicked Israel from its plunge to ruin and to turn the nation back to the Lord. Amos preached a potent message of reproof and judgment.

SUMMARY OF AMOS

The first section of Amos's message (1:1–2:16) finds the prophet pronouncing judgment on six nations that were located around Israel. God pronounced judgment on those nations for their many sins, especially those that hurt God's own people. (The phrase "for three transgressions and for four" emphasizes the multiplicity of their sins.) Why would Amos include these words of judgment in his message of warning to the nation of Israel? He probably gave these short messages as a reminder to Israel that God was not blind to the sins of the other nations; that He was both sovereign and powerful over all the peoples of the earth; and that He did remember and take seriously the Abrahamic Covenant in which He said, "I will bless those who bless you, and the one who curses you I will curse" (Gen.

12:3). This first section ends with a similar word of condemnation directed at the people of Judah (2:4–5) for their sinning in light of their knowledge of God's truth. Finally, there is a summary word of judgment against Israel herself (2:6–16) for her many sins, especially her oppression of the righteous within the land.

The second part of Amos's message (3:1–6:15) is made up of three discourses that detail God's charges against Israel. (Each message begins with the exhortation to "hear": 3:1; 4:1; and 5:1.) In his first discourse, Amos assures Israel that God's judgment is coming. He uses the idea of cause and effect; that is, Israel's sins are the cause of this coming judgment. The prophet's second discourse describes the sinful luxury of the nation and the worthlessness of all her religous activities. He then reminds the people that God has been in the process of disciplining them for many years but that so far they have not responded in a positive way. The kinds of disciplinary actions by the Lord were part of the conditions He set forth in the Mosaic Covenant (cf. Amos 4:6–11, with Lev. 26:14–33). Because Israel had not responded in repentance, she was told to "prepare to meet your God" (4:12). In his third discourse, Amos speaks of the terrible, devastating nature of the coming judgment. He prophesies that only ten percent of the people would be left in the land by the time it was all over (5:1–3; 6:1–14). He invites the Israelites to repent and serve the true God, warning them not to continue in their idolatry.

The third division of the book of Amos is a series of five visions the prophet has (7:1–9:10). The first two visions of a locust plague and a devastating fire view the terrible nature of God's judgments (7:1–6). But these judgments were averted through the intercession of the prophet. The third vision is of a plumb line, which reveals how far off Israel was from God's standards. It reveals how much judgment was deserved. The fourth vision of the basket full of ripe fruit emphasizes the immanency of judgment. The idea is that

Ivory of a woman at a window. Amos attacked the nation's sinful luxury.

Amos was a humble individual who had spent most of his life caring for someone else's sheep.

God's judgment could not be delayed much longer. (Judgment came on Israel less than forty years later.) The final vision of the "smitten capitals" pictures the Lord striking the top of the false temple at Bethel. He struck it so hard that it trembled all over and then collapsed on those inside. This pictures a final and complete judgment of the Northern Kingdom. This third main division of Amos also includes an interesting historical portion that records a confrontation between God's prophet and Amaziah, a priest of Israel's false religion at Bethel (7:10–17). If nothing else, these verses clearly reveal that Amos and his message were not welcomed in the Northern Kingdom.

The fourth and final division of this prophecy is an encouraging word about future restoration (9:11–15). Israel is assured that in the great future Day of the Lord the Davidic dynasty will be restored and Israel will return to live permanently on the land promised to her. The people will live in prosperity and blessing. Amos, like most of the prophets, includes a message of hope in the midst of his prophecies of warning and future judgment.

27. Hosea

INTRODUCTION TO HOSEA

Authorship and Date of Hosea

Except for what can be gleaned from the text itself, nothing is known about Hosea. He was probably from the Northern Kingdom, as there are numerous geographic notations in the message (e.g., 4:15; 5:1; 6:8).

His ministry is clearly dated by the reigns of four southern kings (Uzziah, Jotham, Ahaz, and Hezekiah) and Jeroboam II of the North (1:1). 750 B.C. would be a reasonable date for this prophecy.

Israelite remains at Samaria. Hosea calls the Northern Kingdom by several names, including Samaria.

Basic Outline of Hosea

Hosea

I. The Unfaithful Wife (chaps. 1–3)

II. The Unfaithful People (chaps. 4–14)

Important Data About Hosea

1. Key Word: God's love for Israel
2. Key Chapter: 2—A description of love
3. Key Verses: 1:2–9; 2:5–8; 3:1–5
4. Key Characters: Hosea and Gomer
5. Meaning of "Hosea": Name derives from God's faithful prophet
6. Geography of Hosea: Israel

Purpose of Hosea

This prophecy was God's last voice to the Northern Kingdom of Israel before its destruction. It was a gracious attempt to rescue individuals out of the doomed nation. This message of judgment was fulfilled within a few years.

Special Considerations on Hosea

Hosea calls the Northern Kingdom by several names: Israel, Ephraim, and Samaria (e.g., 4:16–17; 5:9–13; 7:1; 10:6–7). Israel, of course, is the usual designation; Samaria was the capital city of the Northern Kingdom and its name symbolized the entire nation; Ephraim is used because the tribe by that name was the most powerful of the tribes in the Northern Kingdom.

Hosea did not minister in pleasant times. Israel was in as bad a spiritual and moral situation as she had ever been. And it was just as bad politically. After the death of Jeroboam II, murder and intrigue were common in Israeli politics. Out of the last six kings on the throne,

only one died a natural death in office (cf. 2 Kings 15:10–30). Morally and spiritually the people were almost completely defiled.

Blood was shed like water until one stream met another and overspread the land with one defiling deluge. Adultery was consecrated as an act of religion. Those who were first in rank were first in excess. People and king lived in debauchery, and the sottish king joined and encouraged the freethinkers and blasphemers of his court. The idolatrous priests loved and shared in the sins of the people. . . . Corruption had spread throughout the whole land; even those places once sacred through God's revelations or other mercies to their forefathers, Bethel, Gilgal, Gilead, Mizpah, Shechem, were especially scenes of corruption or of sin.[1]

The nation had degenerated morally and spiritually so that they were much like the nations Joshua had driven out of the land many centuries before. Hosea was sent, as God's last prophet, into this decaying situation.

For a short period of time Hosea probably

ministered as a contemporary of Amos in the North and Isaiah and Micah in the South.

SUMMARY OF HOSEA

The first major section of the prophecy focuses on the prophet's family situation, which will become a basis for much of Hosea's message to Israel (1:1–3:5). Extreme times often call for extreme or unusual methods. The nation of Israel had heard the words of many of God's prophets, but the messages of these spokesmen for God had fallen on insensitive ears (cf. Dan. 9:6, 10). So God chose to use a rather extreme approach to get the attention of His people. God chose to use His prophet and his family as an object lesson for Israel. Hosea's family, or more specifically, Hosea's relationship with his wife, would become an illustration of God's love for Israel. Hosea would love his wife even though she would be unfaithful to him, just as God loved Israel even though she had been quite unfaithful to Him.

The first word that came to Hosea from God was an unusual one: God commanded him to marry a woman who would prove to be unfaithful in their marriage relationship. The term "wife of harlotry" (1:2) strongly suggests that Gomer (Hosea's wife) was guilty of sexual immorality before the marriage, perhaps being involved as a temple prostitute. The picture of prostitution ("harlotry") is used by Hosea throughout his message (2:2–5; 3:3; 4:10–19; 5:3–4; 6:10; 9:1). It was a motif entirely appropriate for the nation of Israel in her relationship with God. Hosea married Gomer, and she had three children. These children were given names that would say something about God's

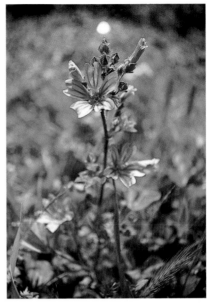

God promises His people new life blossoming like flowers when they return to Him.

relationship with Israel (1:4, 6, 9). The first-born was named *Jezreel* (a name that carried with it the idea of judgment); the second child born was called *Lo-ruhamah* (a name meaning "no pity," indicating that God would no longer show mercy to His rebellious people); and the third child was given the name *Lo-ammi* (which means "not my people," indicating that God was distancing Himself from Israel). There is some evidence that although the first child was clearly Hosea's the other two were not fathered by him.

Apparently Gomer tired of her marriage to this prophet of God and left him, returning back to her life of immorality (2:2, 5). For a while she lived the "good life" of material pleasure and prosperity. Evidently during this time, Hosea actually helped support his wayward wife (2:8). This, of course, would have accurately paralleled what God had done for Israel, prospering her during the reign of Jeroboam II when she was so deeply involved in idolatry. Evidently Gomer's "good life" came to a terrible end and she ended up being auctioned off as a slave. At this point, God instructed Hosea to go and buy back Gomer and to reinstate her as his wife (3:1–3), which he did. This experience in the life of Hosea was designed to show Israel how deep and unchanging was God's love. It would also serve as a basis for Hosea's preaching ministry.

The second major division of this prophecy is a message to this unfaithful nation that had received so much from the Lord (4:1–14:9). The nation of Israel (the Northern Kingdom) had forsaken her "husband" and had gone after other gods—spiritual adultery. Her forsaking of the Lord had bred a multitude of sins that are enumerated by Hosea—unfaithfulness, swearing, deception, murder, stealing, adultery, rebellion, idolatry, disobedience, pride, stubbornness, and involvement in spiritism (4:1– 2, 10–14, 16; 5:5; 6:8–10). Hosea observes that the leaders who should have been giving good guidance to the people were just as sinful as the people (4:9, 18; 5:1; 7:5; 9:15). The Israelites had heard God's warning again and again. Their lack of response had so hardened them that they would not repent (5:4), which meant judgment was sure. Even though there was no hope for the nation, however, that did not mean individuals within the nation could not turn and get right with the true God. Although Hosea saw that judgment was sure, he was like the other prophets in that he was sure God would restore Israel in the future (14:4–9).

28.
Isaiah

INTRODUCTION TO ISAIAH

Authorship and Date of Isaiah

The prophet Isaiah lived and ministered in Jerusalem, where he was the court preacher. Tradition says that he was the cousin of King Uzziah. Isaiah, whose name means "the Lord saves," was married and had at least two sons (cf. 8:18). According to rabbinic tradition, he was sawed in two by order of the wicked King Manasseh. Isaiah lived when the nation of Assyria was the great power in the Middle East, and he was ministering when Assyria invaded Palestine and took the Northern Kingdom of Israel captive.

Some critics of the Bible have denied that Isaiah wrote all sixty-six chapters of this book. It is claimed that another man (referred to as "Deutero-Isaiah") wrote chapters 40–66. But conservative scholars have answered this theory clearly and convincingly. There is just one human author of this great prophecy.[1]

Isaiah had a long ministry, which began in the year that King Uzziah died (740 B.C.) and continued into the reign of Manasseh (696–642 B.C.). Isaiah probably ministered for

about fifty years, and a date of 740 B.C. is given for this book (1:1).[2]

Purpose of Isaiah

Isaiah was raised up by God to speak of coming judgment on Judah because of her many sins and to reveal the coming of "the servant of the Lord." Isaiah was one of the last prophets who offered the nation (as a nation) the opportunity to repent and avoid a national calamity. He also was among the greatest revealers of truth

Important Data About Isaiah

1. Key Word: Servant of the Lord
2. Key Chapter: 1—An overview of the book
3. Key Verses: 1:2–18
4. Key Characters: Isaiah and Hezekiah
5. Meaning of "Isaiah": Name of the man often called "the evangelical prophet"
6. Geography of Isaiah: Judah

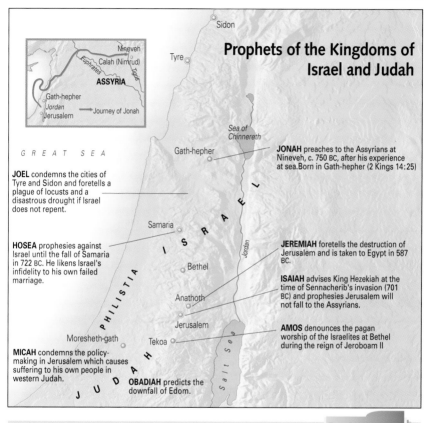

Prophets of the Kingdoms of Israel and Judah

JONAH preaches to the Assyrians at Nineveh, c. 750 BC, after his experience at sea. Born in Gath-hepher (2 Kings 14:25)

JOEL condemns the cities of Tyre and Sidon and foretells a plague of locusts and a disastrous drought if Israel does not repent.

HOSEA prophesies against Israel until the fall of Samaria in 722 BC. He likens Israel's infidelity to his own failed marriage.

JEREMIAH foretells the destruction of Jerusalem and is taken to Egypt in 587 BC.

ISAIAH advises King Hezekiah at the time of Sennacherib's invasion (701 BC) and prophesies Jerusalem will not fall to the Assyrians.

AMOS denounces the pagan worship of the Israelites at Bethel during the reign of Jeroboam II

MICAH condemns the policy-making in Jerusalem which causes suffering to his own people in western Judah.

OBADIAH predicts the downfall of Edom.

Isaiah

Basic Outline of Isaiah

I. Prophecies of Punishment (Chaps. 1–35)

II. Parenthesis for History (Chaps. 36–39)

III. Prophecies of Peace (Chaps. 40–66)

about the person, work, and kingdom of the coming Messiah.

Special Considerations on Isaiah

The primary thrust of Isaiah's message and ministry was toward the Southern Kingdom of Judah (1:1). Some elements of his message applied to Israel before 721 B.C. (the time of Israel's captivity). Also, there is a large section devoted to the foreign nations (13:1–27:13).

Isaiah began his ministry while there were still two kingdoms. During his ministry the Northern Kingdom was taken captive by the Assyrians. Isaiah was a contemporary of Micah in the South and Hosea in the North (and possibly Amos). He was a great help and support to the godly King Hezekiah.

SUMMARY OF ISAIAH

In our basic outline of Isaiah, the first major division has been titled "Prophecies of Punishment" (1:1–35:10). This title is merely a general designation of the content found in this section. The section does contain many words of judgment, but it also includes important truths related to the coming Messiah and His wonderful kingdom.

Isaiah's prophecy begins by focusing on the Southern Kingdom of Judah (1:1–12:6). In the opening chapter there is a brief summary of four essential teachings found in Isaiah, which are developed throughout the book. First, like the other prophets, Isaiah fearlessly points out the sins of God's people. In so many ways they had broken their covenant with God. Isaiah points out their rebelliousness and thankless-ness, their religious formalism and hypocrisy (e.g., 1:2–15, 24–26). Judah at this time was not involved in the gross idolatry of Israel, but she was in grave spiritual danger because she was living by the externals of the law with no real heart for God. A second element in Isaiah's message is the invitation to repent and turn back to the Lord (1:16–20). At this point in history Judah could still come back into a right relationship with the Lord. The third element in his teaching is the warning of coming judgment. Throughout the book Judah is told that judgment will surely come if she fails to turn back to the Lord (1:24–25). Isaiah indicates that time for repentance was running out. The fourth major emphasis in Isaiah is that of coming glory (1:26–27). One of Isaiah's great contributions lies in his revealing of truth related to the Messiah and His kingdom. A great day awaits God's people when the Messiah establishes His reign on the earth.

This focus on Judah (1:1–12:6) continues after the opening chapter with an emphasis on the sin and rebellion of Judah. Although the messianic age will be marvelous (2:1–4), it will only come to a people who walk with the Lord and forsake their sins. The leaders of the nation, as well as many within the nation, are censored for their idolatry, love of luxury, pride, and rebellion (2:5–11; 3:1–26). It is clear that a day of reckoning is coming on them (2:12–22). It is also clear that the Lord had worked diligently with His people. The prophet likens God's efforts to that of a farmer who labors hard trying to produce an excellent harvest of grapes. But in spite of all his work, the harvest produces little of value. Judah and Israel are seen as fruitless nations (5:1–30) facing a bleak future.

Jerusalem in sunlight. "Arise, shine, for your light has come, and the glory of the LORD rises upon you."

Covenant (55:3), a truth that Jeremiah and Ezekiel would develop some years later. Even believing Gentiles will enter the kingdom and enjoy the wonderful reign of Israel's Messiah (55:5; 56:3–8). Isaiah emphasizes that God had to provide salvation because no man could save himself or anyone else (59:16). It is the sin issue that troubled Isaiah as he looked at his people Israel. There were many who were involved in idolatry, with its illicit sex and child sacrifice, as well as in other sins (e.g., 57:1–13). The people generally were involved in the externals of religion but had no real heart for the Lord (58:1–12). There would be no messianic kingdom with Israel in this spiritual condition. But all this will change in the future because the Lord is faithful and characterized by lovingkindness toward Israel. His glory will be seen in Zion.

29. Micah

INTRODUCTION TO MICAH

Authorship and Date of Micah

Micah was from the village of Moresheth, which was located twenty miles southwest of Jerusalem. His name means "who is like Jehovah."

Micah dated his ministry by the reigns of three Southern kings—Jotham, Ahaz, and Hezekiah. A date of 735 B.C. is assigned to this book.

Purpose of Micah

Micah was sent by God to call Judah back to practical righteousness. He particularly denounced the leaders of Judah for oppressing the poor and for using their positions for their own personal gain. He brought a message of coming judgment on Judah. This foreboding message was coupled with a message of hope centered on the coming Messiah.

Special Considerations on Micah

Micah had a word for both the Northern and the Southern Kingdoms (1:1), but it is clear from the content of the book itself that Micah's ministry centered almost exclusively in the south, in the city of Jerusalem.

The ministry of Micah was contemporary with at least two other writing prophets. In the Northern Kingdom, Hosea was illustrating and preaching the love of the Lord, while in the

Important Data About Micah

1. Key Word: Personal righteousness
2. Key Chapter: 3—An attack on Judah's leadership
3. Key Verses: 3:9–12; 5:1–2; 7:18–20
4. Key Characters: Micah and Judah's leaders
5. Meaning of "Micah": Named after the humble prophet whose message is written here
6. Geography of Micah: Judah

turn back to God. Even the revival of Josiah was unable to reverse what Manasseh had done (cf. 2 Kings 21:10–12; 23:26–27; 24:3). The three prophets who spoke for God after the reign of Manasseh could not change the fate of the nation, but they could rescue people individually from the coming events.

King Josiah began his rule in 640 B.C., and his revival began ten years later in 630 B.C. Zephaniah may have played a part in this revival. It should be noted that the revival simply slowed Judah down as she rushed toward judgment.

Basic Outline of Zephaniah

Zephaniah

I. **Coming Judgment on National Judah (Chaps. 1:1–2:3)**

II. **Coming Judgment on Surrounding Nations (Chap. 2:4–15)**

III. **Coming Judgment on National Judah (Chap. 3:1–8)**

IV. **Coming Blessings on All Nations (Chap. 3:9–20)**

SUMMARY OF ZEPHANIAH

The theme of Zephaniah is "the day of the Lord." This phrase occurs seven times in the book (a total of thirteen times if "that day" is included). Several facts are given about the Day of the Lord—it is imminent, it will be a time of terror, it is coming as a judgment for sin, it will be accompanied by great convulsions in nature, it will fall upon all creation, and only a remnant will survive. These statements have both a near and far view (the soon to come Babylonian invasion and the period of tribulation in the distant future).

The first division of Zephaniah's prophecy deals with the coming judgment on the Southern Kingdom of Judah (1:1–2:3). Before the prophet looks at the judgment on Judah, he announces that the entire inhabited earth will face God's judgment. This universal judgment is mentioned by Zephaniah in several places and looks at the ultimate fulfillment of the great future Day of the Lord (1:2, 3, 14–18). The reason for God's discipline of Judah is because of her idolatry (1:4–6). The princes, priests, and the people had knowingly involved themselves in idolatry, turning away willfully from the Lord. While the nation itself had gone so far into sin that it would not turn back to the Lord, individuals within the nation might, and they are invited to do so (2:1–3).

The second section of Zephaniah's message focuses on the coming judgment on certain foreign nations (2:4–15). Philistia, Moab, Ammon, Ethiopia, and Assyria are targeted by the prophet because of their treatment of God's people. However, even some of these foreigners will turn to the Lord.

The third part of this prophecy is once again a word of coming judgment on Judah (3:1–8). Jerusalem has been stubborn and rebellious. Her leaders are seen as greedy, unholy, treacherous, and wicked. And because she has not responded to God's judgments on other nations by learning from them, she too will be punished.

The fourth and final section of this prophecy looks ahead to a future time of salvation and blessing (3:9–20). This section will find its fulfillment when the Messiah establishes His rule on the earth. Fear and failure will be replaced by joy and victory as the King will rule (3:15). God is going to do a great thing for His people. Zephaniah is similar to the other prophets in sounding a hopeful note in the midst of his message of discipline.

As it turned out, the near judgment predicted by Zephaniah came very quickly. In the year 609 B.C. the godly king Josiah died and just four years after that the armies of Babylon invaded and took Judah. Because Judah had not heeded the warnings of Zephaniah and others, she faced the disciplines of God.

32. Jeremiah

INTRODUCTION TO JEREMIAH

Authorship and Date of Jeremiah

Jeremiah was a priest, the son of Hilkiah. Jeremiah lived in the priestly city of Anathoth, which was located a few miles north of the city of Jerusalem.

Jeremiah's ministry lasted about fifty years and spanned the reigns of five kings. His ministry lasted for forty years in Judah (from 626 to 586 B.C.) and beyond that in Egypt, where he ministered to a rebellious remnant.

Purpose of Jeremiah

Jeremiah's messages were given to the kings, rulers, and the people of Judah. His message was heavy with irreversible judgment on Judah. This earned him the characterization of "weeping prophet." Most of the people despised and rejected his message.

Special Considerations on Jeremiah

The historical background to Jeremiah is found in 2 Kings 21–25. As with Zephaniah, Jeremiah's ministry was shaped by events that

Jeremiah

Basic Outline of Jeremiah

I. Introduction (chap.1)

II. Prophecies Against Judah and Jerusalem (Chaps. 2–45)

III. Prophecies Against Various Gentile Nations (Chaps. 46–51)

IV. Supplement (Chap. 52)

Important Data About Jeremiah

1. Key Word: New Covenant
2. Key Chapter: 31—The revelation of the New Covenant
3. Key Verses: 1:4–10; 21:8–10; 31:31–34
4. Key Characters: Jeremiah and the contemporaneous kings of Judah
5. Meaning of "Jeremiah": The name of the steadfast prophet who wrote the book
6. Geography of Jeremiah: Judah and Egypt

Canaanite altar at Megiddo.

had taken place before he became a prophet of God. The total wickedness of Manasseh's reign had doomed the kingdom of Judah. Jeremiah did not have hopes of the nation's repenting. However, he did try to deliver some from judgment and to keep Jerusalem from suffering the horrible destruction that eventually took place.

Jeremiah prophesied during the time when there was a three-cornered struggle for world domination among Assyria, Egypt, and Babylon. Babylon emerged victorious and swept down on Jeremiah's land in 605 B.C.

SUMMARY OF JEREMIAH

The first division of the book of Jeremiah forms the introduction to the prophecy, recording the call of Jeremiah to the prophetic ministry and matters pertaining to that call (1:1–19). God told Jeremiah that he had been set aside as a prophet even before his birth. At the time of his call Jeremiah sensed that he was not adequate for the great task ahead, but the Lord assured him that He would provide for him. Jeremiah was informed that he would face resistance and hostility as he ministered for the Lord, but he was encouraged that these enemies would not overcome him (1:8, 19). Jeremiah was also told that the days of Judah's judgment were very near and that he was to proclaim God's word of judgment faithfully.

The second section of the prophecy makes up the largest portion of the book (2:1–45:5). This section begins with a series of eight messages given in the days of Josiah and Jehoiakim, kings of Judah. These eight

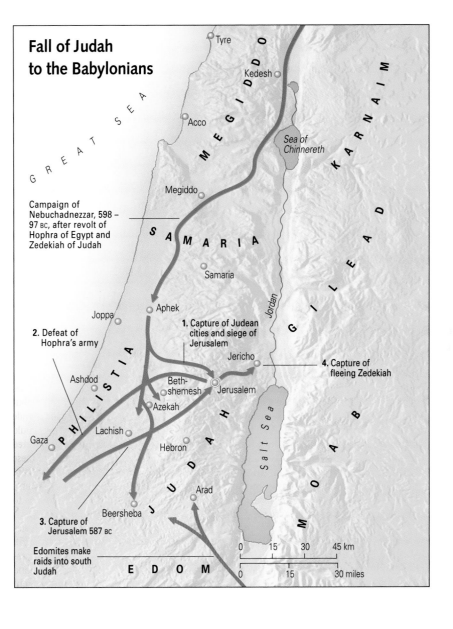

Fall of Judah to the Babylonians

Tyre

Kedesh

MEGIDDO

Acco

KARNAIM

Sea of Chinnereth

GREAT SEA

Megiddo

SAMARIA

Campaign of Nebuchadnezzar, 598 – 97 BC, after revolt of Hophra of Egypt and Zedekiah of Judah

Samaria

GILEAD

Jordan

Aphek

Joppa

1. Capture of Judean cities and siege of Jerusalem

Jericho

4. Capture of fleeing Zedekiah

2. Defeat of Hophra's army

PHILISTIA

Ashdod

Beth-shemesh

Jerusalem

Azekah

JUDAH

Salt Sea

MOAB

Gaza

Lachish

Hebron

Arad

3. Capture of Jerusalem 587 BC

Beersheba

Edomites make raids into south Judah

EDOM

| 0 | 15 | 30 | 45 km |
| 0 | 15 | 30 miles |

messages cover some forty years of ministry and have the same basic emphasis, which is a call for individuals to repent and for the nation to submit to the Babylonians (2:1–20:18). The first message (2:1–3:5) recalls the former love of Israel for the Lord and her present departure from Him. The second message views both Judah and Israel as harlots, guilty of spiritual adultery (3:6–6:30). The third message (7:1–10:25) condemns Judah for her hypocrisy, idolatry, and forsaking of the law. In this message the prophet warns Judah not to trust in the Temple as some sort of good luck charm that would keep away judgment (7:1–11). Evidently many Jews believed that God would not allow "His house" to be destroyed by Gentiles. This idea had brought a false sense of security. The fourth message (11:1–12:17) is a forceful reminder to the people that they had broken their covenant with God and had incurred a curse from Him. Like the rest of the prophets, Jeremiah rebuked God's people for willful violations of their "constitution," which broke the covenant they had made with Him at Mt. Sinai (e.g., 11:1–10; 31:31–32). This strong message of rebuke brought opposition to Jeremiah, as some conspired against him (11:18–23). In the fifth message Jeremiah begins to use signs and symbols in communicating his message (13:1–27). A dirty belt and broken wine jars symbolize judgment and captivity. Drought, famine, the sword, and wild beasts are all indications of God's displeasure and discipline (cf. Lev. 26; Deut. 11) and are found in the sixth message (14:1–15:21). These external disciplines were used by the prophet to point out once again the poor spiritual condition of the nation. The seventh message (16:1–17:27)

God sent Jeremiah to watch a potter at work.

speaks of the great distress to come but also of God's great coming restoration. The eighth message (18:1–20:18) uses the potter and clay as an illustration of the sovereignty of God. Also Jeremiah broke some clay jars in front of the elders of the people, informing them that God was going to break Judah. These messages were personally painful for Jeremiah to deliver inasmuch as he agonized over the coming judgment of his people (cf. 7:1; 20:7–18).

In chapters 21–45 Jeremiah's prophetic message focuses on the coming captivity. His

The Last Days of the Kingdom of Judah

Judean Kings		Prophets	Babylonian Invasions
Mannasseh	697–642	Nahum	
Amon	642–640		
Josiah	640–609	Zephaniah Jeremiah	
Jehoahaz	609–598	Habakkuk Jeremiah Daniel	1st (605) captives taken, including Daniel
Jehoiachin	598–597	Jeremiah Ezekiel	2nd (597) captives taken, including Ezekiel
Zedekiah	597–586	Jeremiah	3rd (586) captives taken, Jerusalem destroyed and the monarchy ends

descriptions of the coming siege and captivity are clear. He exhorts the leaders and the people to avoid needless suffering and pain by submitting to God's rod of discipline, the army of Babylon. If they would submit to God's discipline they would indeed be taken over, but they would avoid much death, destruction, and suffering. Even though his message was true, and eventually verified by the events that took place, Jeremiah was rebuked, rejected, and persecuted for his message (e.g., 26:10–15; 32:1–5). He was viewed as a traitor because of his insistence that Judah submit to the Babylonians and was treated badly because he would not compromise his message of coming judgment. (Note that 21:1–9 and 27:6–15 give a good summary of Jeremiah's

ministry and message.)

This section (from chaps. 21–39) also contains positive messages of rest and deliverance (especially 30:1–33:26) and one of Jeremiah's main messages of hope. His message on the New Covenant (31:31–34) provides valuable truth on the great and grand purposes of God. The New Covenant is a subcovenant of the Abrahamic Covenant (see chart on "God's Covenants with Israel," page 39). The New Covenant is largely occupied with the issue of salvation and is based on the cross of Christ. It was God's declared purpose to save His people Israel from their sins. The New Testament is clear that animal sacrifices could only cover ("atone") sin, but could not remove it (e.g., Heb. 9:11–15, 24–28; 10:4–14). Only the blood of Christ can remove sin and make it possible for sinful men (Israelite or Gentile) to fellowship with a holy God. Jesus spoke of His death as the basis of the New Covenant (Luke 22:20). In Jeremiah 31, Israel and Judah are the subjects of God's salvation, whereas the New Covenant is applied to Gentiles in the church age (2 Cor. 3:1–18; Heb. 8:8–13). Salvation, based on the New Covenant, has come to the Gentiles and in the future will come to the nation of Israel (cf. Dan. 9:24; Rom. 11:25–27). Again in this section (chaps. 40–45) Jeremiah contributes some valuable information about those days and months immediately after the destruction of Jerusalem.

The third major division of the book of Jeremiah contains messages against various Gentile nations (46:1–51:64). For the most part the messages are ones of coming judgment on these nations because of their hostile treatment of God's people. The final section of the prophecy (52:1–34) contains part of Jeremiah's record of the terrible events of 586 B.C. when Jerusalem was destroyed by the Babylonians. This chapter, in combination with 2 Kings 25 and the book of Lamentations, provides a powerful testimony to the accuracy of Jeremiah's predictions of God's judgment.

33. Habakkuk

INTRODUCTION TO HABAKKUK

Authorship and Date of Habakkuk

The prophet does not identify himself either by family lineage or even place of residence. He does refer to himself as a prophet (1:1), and it seems that he was recognized as such since his message would bring a response (2:2). Also the two musical notations might suggest that he was a member of the Temple choir and thus a Levite (3:1, 19).

A date of 609 B.C. is assigned to the book.

Although Habakkuk gives no specific king's reign, the reference to the Chaldeans (Babylonians) indicates that the time of his ministry was probably shortly before the Babylonian invasion of Palestine. It would place the prophecy in the reign of Jehoiakim, shortly after the death of godly King Josiah.[1]

Purpose of Habakkuk

Habakkuk's message weighs the important question how God's patience with sin can be related to His holiness. The dialogue between the prophet and God gives insight

Habakkuk

Basic Outline of Habakkuk

I. Habakkuk and God: The First Dialogue (chap. 1:1–11)

II. Habakkuk and God: The Second Dialogue (chaps. 1:12–2:20)

III. Habakkuk and God: Praise and Prayer (chap. 3:1–19)

Important Data About Habakkuk

1. Key Word: The holiness of God
2. Key Chapter: 1—The revelation of the issue of sin and holiness
3. Key Verses: 1:2, 12; 2:4; 3:2
4. Key Character: Habakkuk
5. Meaning of "Habakkuk": Named after the prophet whose prophecy is written
6. Geography of Habakkuk: Judah, Egypt

into this matter for all time. The sinful, law-breaking people of Judah were a concern to Habakkuk. His distress is registered in his conversation with the Lord.

Special Considerations on Habakkuk

If the date of 609 B.C. is accurate, Judah was only four years away from the Babylonian invasion. The Babylonian empire was on the rise, having taken the Assyrian capital of Nineveh, thus fulfilling the prophecy of Nahum. In 605 B.C., the Babylonians would defeat the Egyptians and Assyrians at the battle of Carchemish. From there they would sweep down and take Jerusalem. Time was just about up for the Southern Kingdom of Judah. It needs to be recalled that the reign of the wicked Manasseh had started Judah down the road to captivity. (See also page 228, "Special Considerations on Zephaniah.")

SUMMARY OF HABAKKUK

The opening section of Habakkuk is a dialogue between the prophet Habakkuk and the Lord (1:1–11). Habakkuk was deeply concerned about the holiness of God. It seemed to him that God's holiness was being compromised by the sin, violence, and lawlessness that was seen everywhere in Judah. The prophet complained that he had been crying out for divine intervention to correct the condition in Judah,

Habakkuk could not understand why God used wicked Babylon to punish his people—and climbed his watchtower to await an answer.

Assyrian kings kept lions for hunting. Daniel was put in a lions' den as a form of execution.

The story shows that God resists proud people but still pursues them in order to bring them to Himself. Chapter 5 records the night when the Babylonian empire came to its end. In October of 539 B.C. the Babylonian king Belshazzar held a feast at which he purposely desecrated the holy vessels from God's Temple in Jerusalem. In response, God caused a hand to appear and write a message of judgment on the wall of King Belshazzar's banquet hall. Daniel came to the banquet hall and interpreted the meaning of the handwriting for the king. The judgment predicted came that very night. This chapter shows that God does indeed raise kings up and take them down as He pleases. Chapter 6 tells the famous story of Daniel in the den of lions. Again Daniel's diligence and faithfulness and God's determination to honor him for it are demonstrated. Daniel was in his early 80s when this incident took place, showing that he was a faithful man throughout his life.

Chapter 7 concludes the second major division of the book of Daniel. This chapter records a vision of four beasts that Daniel received. The vision is quite similar in content to the one in chapter 2. The repetition of information (which was given fifty years after the vision in

The Acropolis, Athens. In Daniel the four-winged, four-headed leopard symbolizes Greece.

chap. 2) is intended to emphasize the certainty of it. In this vision Daniel saw four beasts coming out of the Gentile nations ("the great sea"). The winged lion represents Babylon; the lopsided bear pictures Medo-Persia; and the four-winged, four-headed leopard symbolizes the empire of Greece. Once again, however, the fourth kingdom (the "terrible" beast) is emphasized. Out of the head of this terrible beast came ten horns and then another "little horn." This "little horn" is the first reference to the Antichrist and some important information about him is revealed. The kingdom of the Antichrist will be the last kingdom of man before Christ returns and establishes His kingdom.

The third major division of the book of Daniel gives the prophetic history of Israel as it relates to these Gentile nations (8:1–12:13). Chapter 8 focuses on the second and third empires, those of Medo-Persia and Greece. It reveals how powerfully and suddenly the Medo-Persian empire (the ram in the vision) is destroyed by Greece (the male goat in the vision). Chapter 9 is clearly one of the most important prophetic chapters in the Old Testament. The first part of the chapter records the impassioned prayer of Daniel for his people

The Prophetic Calendar and Daniel's "Times of the Gentiles"

ABRAHAM

The Old Testament Era

605 BC

Babylon

Medo-Persia

2000 YEARS

Greece

Rome I

The Present Church Age

? YEARS

Rome II

7 years Tribulation

Millennium

1000 YEARS

Kingdom of the Son of Man

Rapture of the Church

Second Coming of Christ

E
T
E
R
N
I
T
Y

NEW HEAVEN AND EARTH

Israel. Daniel knew that the prophet Jeremiah had clearly predicted that the captivity of Judah would last for seventy years. He also knew that it would be just two or three years before the time was up. He did not see God doing anything to fulfill His word, and so cried out to God to restore the people and the city of Jerusalem, with its Temple. Daniel 9:24–27 is known as the "Seventy Weeks Prophecy." This important prophecy reveals that God would have 490 years of special dealings with Israel, during which time He would accomplish six important things (9:24). These matters include the redemption and the restoration of Israel and the establishment of Messiah's kingdom. The basis for what He said He would do is the cross of Jesus Christ. The actual fulfillment of most of these matters has yet to take place. The 490 years would be divided into three divisions with the last division being seven years in length. This last seven years is still future and is commonly called the Tribulation period. In interpreting this key prophecy it must be remembered that Israel, not the church of Jesus Christ, is the subject of the prophecy.

Chapters 10 through 12 record the final vision of Daniel, given to him when he was about 85 years old. This vision focuses in great detail on events during the days of the third kingdom of Greece. It also includes comforting words of assurance to Daniel and God's people that the time of resurrection and rewarding is ahead. The book of Daniel is clear that God is the covenant-keeping God.

35. Ezekiel

INTRODUCTION TO EZEKIEL

Authorship and Date of Ezekiel

Ezekiel, whose name means "strengthened by God," was born about 622 B.C. in the land of Judah. He was probably around twenty-five years old when he was taken to Babylon in the second deportation. Like Jeremiah, Ezekiel was a priest who was called by God to be a prophet also (Ezek. 1:1–3).

Ezekiel was taken captive to Babylon in 597

The shepherds of Israel were not looking after their flock—so God promised to be their shepherd.

B.C. He gives the beginning of his prophetic ministry as being in the fifth year of King Jehoiachin's captivity (593 B.C.). His final prophecies were given in the year 570 B.C. (cf. 29:17). Therefore, the date of this book would be somewhere about 570 B.C.

Purpose of Ezekiel

Because Ezekiel was in Babylon when he began his prophetic ministry, it is clear that the captives of Judah residing in Babylon heard his messages. His messages informed his listeners about the impending and final judgment coming at the hands of the Babylonians. He also told of days of glory and hope in the future. Although Ezekiel settled with the group of captives who were located in one of the Jewish settlements near the river Chebar (1:1), his messages were not confined to these people. Many of his words were aimed at the

Important Data About Ezekiel

1. Key Word: Coming judgment and restoration
2. Key Chapter: 36—Restoration after judgment
3. Key Verses: 2:1–7; 36:16–28
4. Key Characters: Judeans in Judah and Babylon
5. Meaning of "Ezekiel": Named after its chief person and author
6. Geography of Ezekiel: Judah and Babylon

Basic Outline of Ezekiel

Ezekiel

I. Introduction: Ezekiel's Commission (chaps. 1–3)

II. Prophecies of Judgment on Judah (chaps. 4–24)

III. Prophecies of Judgment on Gentiles (chaps. 25–32)

IV. Prophecies of Restoration for Israel (chaps. 33–39)

V. Prophecies of Reestablishment for Israel (chaps. 40–48)

Jews who still resided in Judah and remained in their hardened unbelief.

Special Considerations on Ezekiel

Ezekiel lived in Babylon during those final days of the Southern Kingdom of Judah. It is important to note that chapters 1–24 of Ezekiel were given before the final overthrow and destruction of Jerusalem in 586 B.C. These chapters speak of the sin and unbelief of Judah and are very stern pronouncements. But after the fall of Jerusalem in 586 B.C., Ezekiel's messages change dramatically to prophecies of

In Ezekiel's vision water flowed from the Temple to the Dead Sea, making it fresh and full of life.

hope and consolation (chaps. 33–48). The ministry of Ezekiel pivots on that key historical event of the fall of Jerusalem.

SUMMARY OF EZEKIEL

The first section of Ezekiel's prophecy records the call and commission of the prophet (1:1–3:27). Ezekiel records his vision of the glory, power, and majesty of God, which accompanied his call. When God called Ezekiel to minister as His prophet, He informed him that he was being sent to a stubborn, hardened, rebellious nation. His ministry would not be well received when he spoke of judgment. But Ezekiel was to view himself as a watchman. A watchman is obligated to do one basic thing, and that is to sound the alarm. He is not responsible for the response to the alarm.

The second section of the prophecy contains messages of judgment on Judah. These messages were delivered during the final few years before the destruction of Jerusalem in 586 B.C. One of the unique aspects to Ezekiel's ministry was the large number of visual aids he used in his preaching. This attracted the interest of people who had grown tired of listening to the prophets of God. But the message (with or without visual aids) was the same—judgment was coming very soon on Judah because of her sin. The people in captivity knew full well that judgment had come. But the Jews still living in Judah assumed it was just the wicked Jews whom God had shipped off to Babylon. They refused to acknowledge that they were sinful covenant breakers. In fact, both Jeremiah and Ezekiel suggest that God preserved the righteous of

Judah from the times of terrible judgment by taking them to Babylon. The wicked were left in Judah to await the coming judgment.

This coming judgment is detailed in four signs found in 4:1–5:4. Using a variety of attention-getting devices, Ezekiel illustrates the completeness of the coming devastation on Judah. In case anyone should wonder why this judgment was coming, the prophet gives three messages of explanation (5:5–7:27). One of the primary reasons for the judgment was idolatry. Then Ezekiel was given four visions concerning the idolatry in Judah (8:1–11:25). It is here that Ezekiel was given the important vision of the glory of God departing from the Temple. Through this vision God made clear that He was "moving out" of the Temple, which therefore rendered it no longer sacred. This meant God would not destroy those Gentiles who would invade and plunder this once holy structure. The visions also acted as a warning to the people not to put their trust in the Temple building as some sort of good luck charm. Ezekiel's message of judgment continues as he announces through a variety of signs and parables the coming catastrophe (12:1–19:14). In this section the hopelessness of Judah's situation is underscored when God declares that even if righteous Noah, Daniel, and Job were living in Judah He would still bring judgment. Even the presence of those godly men could not stay His hand of discipline (14:14, 20). Ezekiel then targets Jerusalem and the people who lived there. God was definitely going to war against the city (21:1–3) and against the wicked leaders of the nation (22:26–31).

The third major division of the book consists of prophecies of judgment on Gentile nations (25:1–32:32). The nations of Ammon, Moab, Edom, Philistia, Egypt, and Babylon are included in the peoples who will be punished. Once again the warning of the Abrahamic Covenant is heard in these messages as God centuries before declared that He would bless those who blessed Israel and curse those who cursed His people. (See page 98, "Israel and the Nations" for a discussion of these and other nations that had relationships with Israel.)

Following his messages of judgment on Judah and the Gentile nations, Ezekiel looks ahead, in the fourth major section of his book, to the glorious days of restoration (33:1–39:29). According to Ezekiel, Israel had a great future. He speaks of a twofold restoration of the nation. First, Israel would be restored politically and geographically. Although this restoration might appear to be a natural phenomenon, God Himself will bring scattered Israel back to the land of the covenant. This will take place in the "latter days" (34:11–16, 25–30; 37:24–28; 38:8, 16; 39:25–29). Following this physical-geographic restoration there will be a second restoration. This will be the spiritual restoration of the nation back to the Lord God (36:25–27; 37:14, 23–28; 39:22). The order of the restoration is clear—first physical and then spiritual. As He did throughout her history, God will use Gentile nations to accomplish His purposes in the life of Israel (36:19–24; 38:1–39:22).

This monumental menorah stands in Jerusalem as a witness to the return of the Jews to Israel, the land of the covenant, in the "latter days".

Important Data About Zechariah

1. Key Word: The coming Messiah
2. Key Chapter: 14—Messiah's advent
3. Key Verses: 12:10; 14:1–4
4. Key Characters: Zechariah and the people of Israel
5. Meaning of "Zechariah": Named for the prophet
6. Geography of Zechariah: Judah

Special Considerations on Zechariah

Zechariah began his ministry about two months after Haggai spoke to the people about their neglect of the Temple.

SUMMARY OF ZECHARIAH

Zechariah begins his prophecy with a short history lesson. He reminds the people of Israel that their forefathers had paid a high price for their sin. They had disobeyed the law, rejected the reproof of the prophets, and as a result had suffered in exile. If Israel wanted to experience the blessing of the Lord, then Israel must turn from sin to the Lord (1:2–7).

The first major section of Zechariah's prophecy is his "night visions" (1:7–6:8). He received all eight of these visions in one night. These visions contain a great variety of information about Israel's future. The visions are highly symbolic and as a result Zechariah needed help from an interpreting angel in order to understand them. In the first vision,

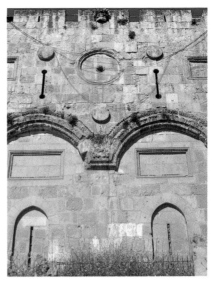

The Golden Gate, Jerusalem, believed by some to open only when Jesus returns.

where the prophet sees a man standing among some myrtle trees, Israel's place of subjection under the Gentile nations is in view. The vision also communicates the assurance that God will someday end Gentile domination (1:8–17). The second vision of the four horns and the four craftsmen communicates the same basic truths as those found in Daniel 2 and 7, information concerning the basic course of Gentile world powers (1:18–21). The third vision (2:1–13) looks ahead to that wonderful time when Messiah will be present, Jerusalem rebuilt, and Israel becomes a channel of blessing. In the key fourth vision, Zechariah sees Joshua the high priest in filthy garments standing before the Lord (3:1–10).

Joshua represents the nation of Israel in its priestly status. Because Israel was filthy in her sin, the question arises regarding how God can do anything for such a wicked, backslidden people. The answer given in this vision is that someday God will step in and give His people clean robes (righteousness) and reestablish them as a priestly nation (the "turban" represents that role). The fifth of the night visions is of a candlestick and olive trees. The olive trees provide an unending supply of oil to the candlesticks. This symbolizes their divine enablement for service, answering the question of where Israel will get the empowerment for this ministry to the Lord. It is interesting to observe the close relationship between this vision and the "two witnesses" in Revelation 11:4. The sixth vision of the flying scroll represents the judgment and removal of sinners in the kingdom of Messiah (5:1–4). The woman in the ephah speaks of the removal of corrupt religion in the future (5:5–11). The final night vision of the prophet Zechariah refers to the Gentile invasions of Israel that will wake the nation (6:1–8). The first major section of Zechariah ends with the coronation of Joshua the high priest. Joshua pictures the day when Messiah the great king-priest will appear and rule (6:9–15).

The second major division of Zechariah contains four messages that came out of questions and events in Zechariah's day (7:1–8:23). For example, in the first message (7:1–7), Zechariah is asked by fellow Jews if they should continue to fast in the fifth month and in the seventh month. These fasts were not given in the law to observe, but rather had been in remembrance of their suffering that came about because of the fall of Jerusalem. Zechariah's response is rather pointed as he made clear that they mourned and fasted over these judgments but not over the sin that had caused them. He exhorts them to mourn over the sin that caused these events and not to fast because of the events themselves. The messages, however, do promise restoration (8:1–8), encouragement (8:9–17), and the hope of Messiah's presence (8:18–23).

The final section of the prophecy has the "two burdens" (9:1–14:21), or weighty messages. These two burdens look at the effect of Gentile world movements on the nation of Israel, especially during the great Day of the Lord. Generally, the first burden focuses on the first advent of the Messiah and the second emphasizes the second advent.

The scope of the subject matter makes Zechariah fit the pattern of the "major prophets". He speaks of the times of the Gentiles, the coming Day of the Lord, the coming of Israel's Messiah, and the glorious days of the kingdom. To a people recently returned from captivity, who felt powerless and vulnerable before their enemies, these messages were messages of hope. God was not finished with them. They did have a future that was a glorious one.

38. *Malachi*

INTRODUCTION TO MALACHI

Authorship and Date of Malachi

The author simply calls himself Malachi, with no further information (1:1). The name Malachi means "my messenger," and this has caused some to believe that it is not a proper name, but simply a title for the prophecy. But most likely it is a proper name, as it would be most unusual for this book to be preserved without giving the

A modern Jordan baptism. Jesus quoted from Malachi in referring to John the Baptist.

name of the author. Malachi was the last of the prophets sent to the remnant at Jerusalem. Tradition has it that he was a member of the Great Synagogue organized by Nehemiah.

In contrast to Haggai and Zechariah, Malachi does not give the date of his prophecy. But certain internal evidence helps us arrive at a date of about 430 B.C. Malachi probably ministered at the same time as Nehemiah. They addressed similar issues. For example, the Temple was completed but being misused (cf. Mal. 1:7–10 with Neh. 3:10); there was corruption in the priesthood (cf. Mal. 1:7–2:9 with Neh. 13:1–9); there was some intermarriage

with the heathen (cf. Mal. 2:11–16 with Neh. 13:23–28); and there was neglect of the offerings of God (cf. Mal. 3:8–12 with Neh. 13:10–13). Malachi's ministry would fit very well into the time just after Nehemiah or perhaps into the time when Nehemiah was absent for a short time from Jerusalem (cf. Neh. 13:6).

Purpose of Malachi

Malachi spoke to the priests, leaders, and people who lived in Jerusalem. Although they were his primary concern, there was probably a larger circle of people who were influenced by his message. A proper view of God was Malachi's great burden. If the people took God seriously, then their sinful ways would be corrected.

Special Considerations on Malachi

The book was written in postexilic times when Israel had been back in her land for about one hundred years. The people of Haggai's day and

Important Data About Malachi

1. Key Word: The fear of the Lord
2. Key Chapter: 1—Exposure of irreverence
3. Key Verses: 1:6–13
4. Key Characters: The priests and people of Judah
5. Meaning of "Malachi": Derived from the author-prophet
6. Geography of Malachi: Judah

the people of Malachi's day were quite different spiritually. Haggai ministered to people who were far more responsive to the things of the Lord. During the one hundred years Israel had once again started to backslide. Outwardly Israel seemed to be doing well spiritually, but inwardly she was drifting away from her spiritual moorings. Malachi came as the last voice from God before the centuries of silence. His rebukes were specific and pointed.

SUMMARY OF MALACHI

The first section of Malachi's prophecy is a declaration of God's love for Israel (1:1–5). Malachi's message begins with the word "the oracle burden of the word of the Lord" (1:1). This title immediately reveals that this is a burdensome message and not a message of comfort. God reminds Israel that He loves her, and this love is seen in that He selected and preserved Israel for Himself.

The second part of the prophecy focuses on the unfaithful priests (1:6–2:9). The priests were supposed to bring the people close to the Lord, but instead they were guilty of serious sins themselves. They were bringing blemished offerings to the Lord (cf. 1:6–9 with Deut. 15:21), kindling strange fire (1:10), defiling the name of Jehovah before the Gentiles (1:11–14) and disregarding the law of God (2:1–9).

In the third division of the book, Malachi looks at the backslidden people (2:10–4:3). They were guilty of such sins as divorcing their Jewish wives to marry foreigners and refusing to pay their tithes. But the key to understanding Malachi's message is to see the underlying cause for Israel's many sins: she had lost her fear and reverence of the Lord God. The fear of the Lord involved an awe as well as a commitment to Him as revealed in obedience and loyalty.[1] In the Scriptures, the fear of the Lord is seen as an important deterrent to sin (cf. Ex. 20:20; Prov. 16:6). Malachi uses the word *fear* seven times (1:6; 2:5; 3:5; 4:2).

Before Malachi concludes his message, he informs Israel that God will be sending His messenger, who will prepare for the coming of the Messiah (3:1–3; 4:4–6). With the promise of this coming messenger, the Old Testament closes and the voice of God becomes silent for some four hundred years. The silence would not be broken until the angel Gabriel announced to the old priest Zacharias that he would father a son—a son who would fulfill the promise of Malachi (cf. Luke 1:13–16).

ℰ𝒩otes

Chapter 1:
Introduction to the Old Testament

1. Merrill C. Tenney, *Interpreting Revelation* (Grand Rapids: Eerdmans, 1957), 101–16.
2. A. W. Tozer, *The Knowledge of the Holy* (New York: Harper & Row, 1961), 7.

Chapter 3: Genesis

1. Edward J. Young, *Studies in Genesis One* (Nutley, N.J.: Presbyterian and Reformed, 1964), 6.
2. Howard F. Vos, *Genesis* (Chicago: Moody, 1982), 10.
3. Weston W. Fields, *Unformed and Unfilled* (Nutley, N.J.: Presbyterian and Reformed, 1976), 162–63.
4. John C. Whitcomb, *The Early Earth,* rev. ed. (Grand Rapids: Baker, 1986), 56.
5. Ibid., 146, and Fields, *Unformed,* 87.
6. Vos, *Genesis,* 14.
7. John C. Whitcomb and Henry M. Morris, *The Genesis Flood* (Philadelphia: Presbyterian and Reformed, 1961), 243.
8. John C. Whitcomb, *The Early Earth,* rev. ed. (Grand Rapids: Baker, 1986), 118–40.
9. Davis A. Young, *Christianity and the Age of the Earth* (Grand Rapids: Zondervan, 1982).
10. Arthur Custance, *Without Form and Void* (Brockville, Ont.: Arthur Custance, 1970).
11. John C. Whitcomb, *The Early Earth,* rev. ed. (Grand Rapids: Baker, 1986); Henry Morris, *Scientific Creationism* (San Diego: Creation-Life, 1981).
12. *Ibid.,* 10.
13. *Ibid.,* 1–35.
14. David Barker, "The Waters of the Earth: An Exegetical Study of Psalm 104:1–9," *Grace Theological Journal* 7, no. 1 (Spring 1986): 57–80.
15. Allen P. Ross, "The Table of Nations in Genesis 10—Its Content," *Bibliotheca Sacra* 138 (January–March 1981): 22–34.
16. Allen P. Ross, "The Dispersion of the Nations in Genesis 11:1–9," *Bibliotheca Sacra* 139 (April–June 1981): 119–33.
17. J. Dwight Pentecost, *Things to Come* (Grand Rapids: Dunham, 1964), 74.
18. John F. Walvoord, *The Millennial Kingdom* (Findlay, Ohio: Dunham, 1963), 150.
19. Walter C. Kaiser, *Toward an Old Testament Theology* (Grand Rapids: Zondervan, 1981), 93.
20. Walvoord, *Millennial Kingdom,* 150–52.
21. Kaiser, *Old Testament Theology,* 94.
22. Eugene H. Merrill, *A Historical Survey of the Old Testament* (Grand Rapids: Baker, 1980), 76.
23. Louis Berkhof, *Systematic Theology* (London: Banner of Truth, 1941), 48.
24. Ibid., 49.
25. Charles R. Gianotti, "The Meaning of the Divine Name YHWH," *Bibliotheca Sacra* 142 (January–March 1985): 38–51.
26. Walter C. Kaiser Jr., *Toward an Old*

Testament Theology (Grand Rapids: Zondervan, 1981), 107.

27. Ibid., 98.

28. Charles Ryrie, *A Survey of Bible Doctrine* (Chicago: Moody, 1977), 28–29.

29. Vos, *Genesis,* 105.

30. Howard Vos, *Genesis* (Chicago: Moody, 1982), 15–16; John J. Davis, *Moses and the Gods of Egypt* (Winona Lake, Ind.: BMH, 1971), 56.

31. Eugene Merrill, *A Historical Survey of the Old Testament* (Grand Rapids: Baker, 1980), 15.

32. Merrill F. Unger, *Introductory Guide to the Old Testament* (Grand Rapids: Zondervan, 1956); Oswald T. Allis, *The Five Books of Moses* (Philadelphia: Presbyterian and Reformed, 1949); E. J. Young, *An Introduction to the Old Testament* (Grand Rapids: Eerdmans, 1969).

33. Vos, *Genesis,* 7.

Chapter 4: Exodus and Leviticus

1. John J. Davis, *Moses and the Gods of Egypt* (Winona Lake, Ind.: BMH Books, 1971), 45–48.

2. Eugene Merrill, *A Historical Survey of the Old Testament* (Grand Rapids: Baker, 1980), 101–2.

3. J. N. Oswalt, "Chronology of the Old Testament," in *International Standard Bible Encyclopedia* (Grand Rapids: Eerdmans, 1949), 1:677.

4. Charles H. Dyer, "The Date of the Exodus Reexamined," *Bibliotheca Sacra* 140 (July–September 1983): 559:235.

5. John J. Davis, *Moses and the Gods of Egypt* (Winona Lake, Ind.: BMH, 1971), 30.

6. Dyer, "The Date of the Exodus Reexamined."

7. Davis, *Moses and the Gods of Egypt,* 31.

8. Eugene Merrill, *A Historical Survey of the Old Testament* (Grand Rapids: Baker, 1980), 107.

9. Davis, *Moses and the Gods of Egypt,* 19.

10. Samuel J. Schultz, *Leviticus* (Chicago: Moody, 1983), 54.

Chapter 6: Joshua

1. Merrill F. Unger, *Archaeology and the Old Testament* (Grand Rapids: Zondervan, 1960), 175.

2. Ibid., 172–75.

3. John J. Davis, *Conquest and Crisis* (Winona Lake, Ind.: BMH, 1969), 50.

Chapter 7: Judges and Ruth

1. Leon Wood, *Distressing Days of the Judges* (Grand Rapids: Zondervan, 1975), 10.

Chapter 8: 1 Samuel

1. J. Carl Laney, *First and Second Samuel* (Chicago: Moody, 1982), 8.

2. Walter C. Kaiser, *Toward an Old Testament Theology* (Grand Rapids: Zondervan, 1981), 145.

3. Leon Wood, *Distressing Days of the Judges* (Grand Rapids: Zondervan, 1975), 26.

4. Kaiser, *Old Testament Theology,* 148–49.

Chapter 9: 2 Samuel

1. J. Carl Laney, *First and Second Samuel* (Chicago: Moody, 1982), 99.

Chapter 10: 1 Kings

1. Wayne Brindle, "The Causes of the Division of Israel's Kingdom," *Bibliotheca Sacra* 141

(July–September 1984): 231.
2. Ibid., 224–27.
3. Ibid., 229.

Chapter 12: 1 and 2 Chronicles
1. Gleason L. Archer, *A Survey of Old Testament Introduction* (Chicago: Moody, 1964), 389.
2. W. F. Albright, "The Biblical Period," in *The Jews: Their History,* ed. Louis Finkelstein (New York: Schocken, 1970), 49.
3. Irving L. Jensen, *Jensen's Survey of the Old Testament* (Chicago: Moody, 1978), 211.

Chapter 13: Ezra and Esther
1. Paul N. Benware, *Ambassadors of Armstrongism* (Fort Washington, Pa.: Christian Literature Crusade, 1984), 90.

Chapter 15: Hebrew Poetry
1. Samuel J. Schultz, *The Old Testament Speaks* (New York: Harper & Row, 1970), 279.
2. Eugene Merrill, *A Historical Survey of the Old Testament* (Grand Rapids: Baker, 1980), 232.
3. Ibid., 232.
4. John Walton, *Chronological Charts of the Old Testament* (Grand Rapids: Zondervan, 1981), 75.

Chapter 16: Job
1. Roy B. Zuck, *Job* (Chicago: Moody, 1978), 8–9.
2. Merrill F. Unger, *Introductory Guide to the Old Testament* (Grand Rapids, Zondervan, 1950), 379.

Chapter 17: Psalms
1. Samuel J. Schultz, *The Old Testament Speaks* (New York: Harper & Row, 1970), 286.

Chapter 19: Ecclesiastes
1. Walter Kaiser Jr., *Ecclesiastes: Total Life* (Chicago: Moody, 1979), 24–29. Ardel B. Caneday, "Qoheleth: Enigmatic Pessimist or Godly Sage?" *Grace Theological Journal* 7, no. 1 (Spring 1986): 21–56.

Chaper 20: Song of Solomon
1. Paige Patterson, *Song of Solomon* (Chicago: Moody, 1986), 14–17. Weston Fields, "Early Jewish and Medieval Interpretation of the Song of Songs," *Grace Theological Journal* 1, no. 2 (Fall 1980): 221–31.
2. Patterson, *Song of Solomon,* 17–27.
3. S. Craig Glickman, *A Song for Lovers* (Downers Grove, Ill.: InterVarsity, 1978), 173–87.
4. John Sampey, "Song of Songs," in *International Standard Bible Encyclopedia* (Grand Rapids: Eerdmans, 1949), 5:2833.

Chapter 21: Lamentations
1. Irving L. Jensen, *Jeremiah and Lamentations* (Chicago: Moody, 1966), 121.
2. C. F. Keil, *Biblical Commentary on the Old Testament: The Prophecies of Jeremiah,* trans. James Kennedy (Edinburgh: T. and T. Clark, 1874), 1:16.
3. Samuel J. Schultz, *The Old Testament Speaks* (New York: Harper & Row, 1970), 341.